WHAT DOES GOD EXPECT OF ME?

How to Release the Supernatural Character of God in Your Life

Gail Edward Craig

WHAT DOES GOD EXPECT OF ME?

How to Release the Supernatural Character of God in Your Life

Gail Edward Craig

ISBN-13: 978-1978304833
ISBN-10: 1978304838

FOREWARD

Are you ready for an adventure? Then read this book!

In his powerful new book, "WHAT DOES GOD EXPECT OF ME," my dear friend, Pastor Gail Craig, issues a clarion call to not only awaken this generation to the reality that God has a plan for them, but also that God expects believers to be ready to give an answer for the Gospel. We must stop wavering between opinions and realize that this is OUR NOW. Every single page of this book declares truth in a day and age where this generation is searching for answers. This book teaches us that we must be ready, filled with the Spirit of God, and His overwhelming joy. Get ready to be stirred to allow God to have complete control of not only our everyday, but we must live as if tomorrow will never arrive.

I truly believe that we are on the verge of the greatest spiritual awakening that the world has ever seen. How will this happen? It will happen when this generation realizes that they are not an "oops," or an "accident," but those who are destined to "cry aloud and spare not," (Isaiah 58:1)! Now is the time for the sleeping church to arise to, and declare freedom, hope, and passionate pursuit of Jesus as never before.

This book is not just a good read, but also a war manual for you to survive the battle coming at you every day in the secular culture in which we now live. We must arise and lead in the land of wandering saint and salt-less church. Hosea 4:6 declares, "My people are destroyed from their lack of knowledge...." This book will not only give you the answers that you have been searching for, but it will also require that you answer these questions:

- Is your wavering causing wandering?
- Has culture corrupted your spirit?
- Will you allow God to pour His amazing love into your heart, then share it with others?
- Will you be a light in darkness?
- Can God trust you with His Spirit?
- Are you ready to be filled with Joy?

God requires only one thing: all of you. When God's sovereignty takes control of our lives, then we no longer are moved by opinion, personalities, or catchy doctrine, but simply by the will of God. YOU are the voice that the world has been waiting on to change the dialogue! I challenge you to hide away and grow as you read this book. Your greatest moments of spiritual training will not come while standing on the platform of ministry, or in the office of the elite, but in the cave and in the wilderness. This is your moment to grow in God as never before! It is time to give an account for the "dash" on your future tombstone!

Let the Remnant arise and lead the awakening!
PAT SCHATZLINE, Evangelist and Author,
Remnant Ministries International

Index

INTRODUCTION

At the age of twelve, I was born again, having received Jesus Christ as my Savior and Lord. I grew up one of five children, as a "pastor's kid" in a third generation Minister's (Pastor's) home. My parents served in Pastoral Ministry for over fifty years. This unique relationship and heritage gave me great blessings and insights in the Word of God and the Person of the Holy Spirit.

At an "altar of prayer" following a Sunday evening Worship Gathering at my father's church, God called me into full-time vocational Ministry. This encounter transformed my life and I began a journey of intimate, Spirit-filled relationship with "Almighty God," which continues to this day!

Along the journey of preparation through College, attaining Ministerial Credentials, serving as Youth Pastor on a multiple Church Staff, itinerate Evangelism and then as Lead Pastor, I had often wondered "What God Expected of Me?" as a believer. This question stirred up a passion to find answers and bring spiritual understanding. Having experienced God through daily times of prayer and continual encounters in His presence, studying the truth of His Word, laying down my life for Him, and serving The Kingdom of God, He began to bring inspiration and revelation of what "God Expects of Me."

We live in an age of troubling times, troubled people and troubled values. The world challenges the very core of every Christian believer. The scriptural perspective you will discover and receive from this book will inspire and motivate you to a deeper understanding of how believers are to live in this present world. What God Expects of Believers - He empowers with His Holy Spirit, so that you may fulfill His desire for you. His ability to help you do what you don't have the ability to do, will infuse your life! You can live in What God Expects and Empowers. Insights, inspiration, and revelation are before you. As you read and study the messages of this book, please be open and ready for God to stir, challenge and bless your life!

Gail E. Craig
Lead Pastor
Freedom Church

Chapter One

Gather the Harvest

I find myself meditating on God's expectation for believers after watching the news, perhaps just as you have. When I see all the things going on in the world, Matthew 24 comes to mind instantly. The Bible warns of wars and rumors of wars in the last days, but also tells us we are to see that our hearts are not troubled by the news (verse 6). As children of the Most High God (who still has all things in control), we believers do not need to give in to fear or be full of anxiety. There's no doubt we are living in a very interesting day with many kinds of threats in our world and in the world system. When the Bible speaks of "the world," it is referring to the world's system of sin, destruction, defeat, despair, and distrust.

The world today is no different from how it was in Jesus' day. It is just that we have more sophisticated communication, weaponry, and instant media newscasts showing us what is happening around the world. The technology today is greater, but the problems of the world haven't changed. The culture when Jesus came on the scene was one of tyranny rule. The Roman Empire was tyrannizing all the known world at that time. In Jesus' day, there were terrorist rulers, depravity, national hatreds, poverty, and economic failure just as today. Even then people cried out for peace because of their fear, disease and wars.

When Jesus arrived on the scene, some expected Him to immediately overthrow the Roman government and become a King who would get rid of the tyrants, so they could enjoy peace. But Jesus came to our world to do something quite different, didn't He? He came to die for all mankind so that now in our day, we can have the same peace, power, and anointing that Jesus brought to His day. That is why He sent the Holy Spirit upon us to minister to us. So, you see, the world hasn't changed much. It is still selfish, prideful, and there are still threats to peace. King Solomon said there is really nothing new under the sun, and we can certainly see that is true as far as human nature is concerned.

God gives us precious promises in the Word of God, and one such promise is if sin increases, the grace of God increases even more. **Romans 5:20 states, *"Where sin abounds the grace of God much more abounds."*** When there are problems and unrest in the world, we have the grace (ability) of God to help us to do what we otherwise would not have the ability to do, and that grace is stronger, mightier, and more incredible in these last days, as God pours out His Spirit upon all flesh.

As believers, we need to shift our focus from all the struggles in this world and begin praising God for pouring out His anointing into the midst of it, for that is the promise of the Word to us. God's anointing brings peace, contentment, love, grace, power, and harmony to our lives. God expects our response as believers to be focusing on eternity, not just looking at the present moment.

"And as Moses lifted up the serpent in the wilderness, even so must the Son of Man be lifted up, that whoever believes in Him [Jesus] should not perish but have eternal life. For God so loved the world [not only the world system but every person in the world who is without Jesus] that He gave His only begotten Son, that whoever believes in Him should not perish but have everlasting life. For God did not send His Son into the world to condemn the world, but that the world through Him might be saved." (John 3:14-17)

The above verses will be foundational for our study of what God expects from believers. Let's pray.

Heavenly Father, make the Word of God alive to us today, send it deep into our hearts. Challenge our hearts with Your expectations of us. In Jesus' mighty Name, amen.

In lieu of the day, age, and the season in which we live, there are some expectations God has of us. I want to look at three of these more closely.

GOD EXPECTS BELIEVERS TO STAND STRONG IN SPIRIT

God's number one expectation for us is that we will stand strong in His Spirit. He does not expect us to stand strong in brute strength or in the might of our own ability. He provides us with a power in the Holy Spirit causing us to be strong, not moved by what we see, knowing the truth of the Word of God, and knowing the season and the time in which we live. We are living in an interesting season, an interesting time in history.

"Season" in the Scripture is defined as the set time of God's favor for believers. We are living in a season where God sent His anointing to minister in a powerful and dynamic way. He sent His Spirit to minister to us, so we can stand strong in the power of God's anointing. God does not expect us to placate the culture, or to play with the system of the flesh, or to cater to the world system or its way of doing things. But He, in this season, has an expectation which is in direct opposition to these things of the world.

We are living in a season when the world draws back and holds back financially. The world in this season has a tendency to hide itself, go hide and protect oneself, do something for self; pull back, or become self-oriented, and doubtful. In this season, the world system steps back, takes a second look, and doubts everything everyone says. When we watch the newscasts and even how the news is reported, we realize most stories are slanted and produce doubt and unbelief. There are many kinds of stresses in our world, and the news is reported from that slant.

But in this season, because it is the set time of God's favor for believers, the Lord has a different expectation for us. It is not to step back, but to step up; it is not to draw back the way the world does, but to step up into the realm of the Holy Spirit and the anointing. It is not to take a back seat to what the devil may be doing, but to step up our prayer life in the anointing of God. God expects His people to step to the forefront, so He can reveal His power in and upon those believers who will touch the lives of others and bring them into the Kingdom of God.

We live in the season of Harvest. We live in a season to release to God, not to hold back from Him. This is not a season to pinch our pennies, but to release finances to God. This is not a time to hold back because we think the economy may soon fail. It is a time to put our trust in God to take care of us. We do that by giving our tithes and offerings into the kingdom of God. This season is not a time of withdrawal but a time of release. It's not a time to hide, but a time to rise up. It is time for us to stand up, not a season for us to back away and be afraid to talk to people about Christ. It is a season to rise up in resurrection power and let the work of God in our lives be made known. That is the season we live in today.

We all have neighbors and people on the job who are filled with fear or apprehension about what is going on in our day. God expects us to stand up in faith, not shrink back because of fear, or the devil. God expects us to be focused on eternity, to sacrifice our lives for peace, if necessary. Knowing Jesus as we do, we also know whatever may happen to us will usher us right into the presence of God anyway. So why shrink back or worry about the dangers in the world today?

Our responsibility, and the expectation of God, is to let others in our day-to-day lives see the strength of faith God provides. They need to know the strength of the Spirit by which we stand. When we walk in joy rather than sorrow and live our life with faith rather than doubt, others around us see our positive outlook. They then begin to wonder what makes us different. The expectation of God for that moment is for us to step up, rise up in His resurrection power, and declare to them who Jesus Christ is in us by standing strong in the Spirit of God!

". . . that He will grant you according to the riches of His glory, to be strengthened with might through His Spirit in the inner man." (Ephesians 3:16)

"Might" as used in this context is translated as *dunamis* (dynamite) power, in connection with the Holy Spirit. Dunamis power is supernatural might, ability and strength of God. We are instructed to stand in that God-given power or might. We are not to stand in our own ability or our own arrogance or pride, but to stand in the anointing of the Holy Spirit who dwells within us, which demonstrates to onlookers we are not afraid of the enemy.

The book of Psalms mentions we ***"will not be afraid of the terror by night, nor the arrow that flies by day, nor the pestilence that walks about by night," (Psalm 91:5).*** We are told not to be afraid of any of it because we possess a supernatural strength in God. This strength is in us by the Holy Spirit and we are enabled to stand strong in the Spirit of God and not be afraid. Praise God!

I ask Him to strengthen you by His Spirit, not a brute strength, but a glorious inner strength. (Ephesians 3:16, The Message Translation)

Also, Colossians 1:11 commands to be ***" strengthened with all might according to His glorious power."*** God's expectation for believers is to stand strong in His

Spirit, letting the anointing of God and His power flow through our life.

You may have noticed a turn in the atmosphere of the world, and that turning is a positive upswing of the anointing of God. Have you sensed it? There's a new empowerment, a new strength, a new vigor coming up inside our spirit, and giving new urgency to the days we are in. We know it is time to stand up and not shrink up, not give in, or give up. Come on, somebody! Walk in the power of the Spirit! This same increased anointing and urgency is being sensed the world over in our day!

GOD EXPECTS BELIEVERS TO BE READY TO GIVE AN ANSWER FOR OUR HOPE.

We are to be ready to give an answer to anyone or anything He brings across our path, by proclaiming Jesus as Lord of our lives and the hope we have in Him. God deposits that hope into us, along with the desire to share that hope with others. We are to be ready to say, "Here is why I have hope when it looks hopeless. Here is why I have faith in the face of faithlessness. Here is why I have joy when it seems the world is in sorrow. His Name is Jesus Christ, the Son of the Living God! He puts faith in my heart and faith in my spirit, so I can walk with Him in perilous times and not be afraid of anything!"

God expects us to give an answer and a reason for the hope in us because there are always people watching our life. They look at us because they can't understand why we are so calm, happy, content; they especially notice we are not stressed out. They are wondering in their minds what makes us different from them. We know what the difference is: it's Jesus Christ and Him crucified, living in us, forgiving us of sin, and He is alive in us in His resurrection power. That is why we have hope.

The expectation of the Lord is to be instantly ready for each opportunity to give an answer. Let's do a little Bible study on this topic.

"But sanctify the Lord God in your hearts and always be ready to give a defense [or an answer] to everyone who asks you, a reason for the hope that is in you, with meekness and fear. (I Peter 3:15)

This verse is not a prayer. It is a command! Peter commands us to sanctify the Lord, because he knew God brings people across our paths who will ask us questions. "Why are you so peaceful with all this chaos going on in the world? Why do you seem so stable? What is it?" We've got to be ready in a moment to declare the victory of God.

This is so strong in my heart! I was talking to someone this week who was right in the middle of a very difficult time. They were feeling incredible pressure because their life seemed to be falling apart. God gave me the opportunity to talk to that individual and share Jesus with them. "Listen, I know someone who can help you. You're under a lot of pressure and stress, and for good reason. There are a lot of things going on in your life. But I have an answer, and His Name is Jesus! If you will receive and trust in Him, He will help you handle all this stress in your life." Be instantly ready to give an answer, to defend the Gospel, and ready to tell others, "I know your answer, and it is not in those things you are seeking in the natural. Your answer is found here in the living Word of God through a personal relationship with Jesus Christ as your Savior."

As you read this, I want to ask you some questions. Are you ready to give an answer to someone who asks you about why you have peace in the middle of the world's chaos and terror? Are you ready to explain to your employer the reason you are still smiling is because you've been on your knees in prayer, reading the Word of God, and God gave you an assurance that we are going to be okay? Are you ready to explain this is why believers still have joy in the midst of pressure? Are you ready to speak what God puts in your mouth? The reason people will ask is because God prepared their hearts in advance, to be receptive, to hear what we will speak to them! A miracle will take place in their life if we will but follow the leading of the Holy Spirit when they ask. God desires to bring them to Himself. The Holy Spirit will be faithful to draw them in, if we will be faithful to step out by faith and share our Good News. Are you catching this in your spirit?

We are ready on a moment's notice to give an answer for our hope. ***"My hope is in You, O Lord. (Psalm 39:7)***. David also spoke of this, ***"I hope in Your Word." (Psalm 119:114)***

"Hope won't disappoint because the love of God has been poured out in our heart by the Holy Ghost which is given unto us." (Romans 5:5)

Our hope is in Christ! We have the love of God and we're filled with His joy, hallelujah? Are you ready to answer any who asks? Get ready because they will ask, for God desires to bring them to us. He gives us opportunity to participate with Him in bringing them into the Kingdom of God. That is what the last day harvest is all about!

I don't think anyone ever thought about what it would take to get the last day harvest launched. We are living in a day, folks, where nuclear weapons are everywhere, and anything could happen any day. Perhaps God is using this time and this season to get people into the kingdom. Luke 21:26 states people's hearts will fail them because of fear of those things coming upon the earth. It is our opportunity to tell them why we are not afraid. "Look, I love and serve Jesus Christ. He is my Lord and He gives me peace in the midst of storms. You can have the same peace I have by believing in Him."

GOD EXPECTS BELIEVERS TO GATHER THE HARVEST

I know this is the heart of God for this day and age. This is the season of harvest for salvation of souls into the kingdom, for healing, for signs, wonders and miracles, for financial blessing upon believing tithers and givers, in order that the Gospel is preached, and souls reached.

I want to insert an astounding statistic here. It used to be that Japan had the lowest percentage of Christians per capita in the world. It was said at one point that only two percent (2%) of Japan's population were evangelized Christians. I don't know Japan's population, but I do know that although Japan is a small nation, its population is huge.

My wife and I have been in Tokyo. We rode the subways and experienced being crammed inside to make room for as many as possible. There are subway attendants wearing white gloves whose job is to push people into the subway until each car is packed so tight no one can move, and they can't possibly get another person inside. I'm telling you that is crowded! We too were pushed into one of those crammed subway cars.

America, on the other hand, used to be number one (#1) per capita for professing Christians serving God. Do you know what has happened now? America's Christians dropped below two percent (2%) per capita! That concerns me! We are seeing other nations in the world sending missionaries to America! I am not kidding you. Revival is breaking out in other countries around the world. Latin American countries have a greater per capita percentage than America! Argentina has almost 70% of their people born-again and/or Spirit -filled! We supposedly are the greatest Christian nation on the face of the earth, and yet we've dropped below two percent who are actually born again, Bible believing Christians!

Do you know what that tells me? We have not been praying enough, we have not been evangelizing our own people enough, and we haven't been talking to our neighbors enough. We must do these things in order to have the power of God moving! God expects us to gather in the harvest while people are seeking to know the truth, and seeking for the reality of God!

We have Upward Basketball on Saturdays in our Church gym. I spend much of my time walking around meeting and talking to parents, and praying with these parents, if necessary. That is one of the reasons for our gym and the reason for outreach activities in the gym. It is to bring people to our campus where the Spirit of God is, where the anointing of God is, and to give us opportunities to talk to them and minister to them, thereby building relationships with unbelievers whose children participate in our church-sponsored sports program for our community.

We have video footage of what goes on in our Community Life Center with testimonials of the powerful things happening in these outreaches. Kids are getting saved in basketball practice because their coach gives them an age-appropriate devotion from the Word of God every week. Our gym is not just for basketball, volleyball, or soccer. No, it's being used as a tool for reaping a harvest into the kingdom of God. Basketball might be the hook we use, but it's the Word of God which brings the Life! Hallelujah, glory to God!

Gathering in the harvest is part of our responsibility, yours and mine, because we are anointed believers.

GOD EXPECTS EVERY BELIEVER TO PRAY FOR HARVEST

"Then Jesus said to His disciples, 'The harvest truly is plentiful, but the laborers are few. Therefore, pray the Lord of the harvest to send out laborers into the harvest." (Matthew 9:37-38)

God sent His one and only Son to harvest the world, not to condemn it but that the world through Him might be saved. In our day, He expects us not only to pray for laborers but to become one of them! It is easy to be an armchair Christian who sits back and prays the Pastor will preach a good message and people will be saved, but then go on our way through the week without talking about Jesus or witnessing to others about Him, and believe we are doing our part by praying for God to bring in the harvest.

Harvest workers start with prayer, but it doesn't end there. Yes, every born-again believer is to be involved with prayer for the lost. We need every person in the body to be praying for the lost and the backsliders who have fallen away from Him. We are to pray for those who have walked away from Him, and ask Him to bring them back into the kingdom and back into the house of God. We are to pray they will be brought into a personal, intimate relationship with Him. Every one of us is to be involved in that.

We also need to pray for laborers, asking God to send someone into their path. I'll guarantee if we start praying for laborers, God will speak to us personally about being that somebody. We cannot have a full burden for the lost without having a heart to tell someone about Jesus. Our heart cries out to let them know, through our witness, about the truth of Jesus and His love for them. We are instructed to pray for gatherers -- reapers -- of the harvest.

"Do you not say there are still four months and then comes the harvest. Behold I say to you, 'lift up your eyes and look at the fields, for they are already white for harvest.'" (John 4:35)

Did you notice it doesn't say there will be a harvest coming, but that harvest time is already here? God has a harvest ready for that person we've talked to and prayed for. This is the appointed season for harvest. If it takes the threat of war to bring someone to Jesus, we are to use that opportunity to speak into their lives. If it takes the threat of terrorism in our front yard and our friends and neighbors are frightened, we are to use the opportunity to bring them to Jesus! It is our privilege to be involved in the gathering of the harvest.

First of all, we are to pray for the harvest. If you will remember back when 9/11 happened, America came together to pray even though most had not been praying collectively before that. After the terrorist act, we began to pray. After the shuttle exploded in the air, we began to pray. This is America's pattern. After things happen we decide we better go to God about it, but by then it is too late for many people. We are commanded to pray the Lord of the harvest will send forth harvesters now!

How many of us have loved ones who need Jesus? We need to pray for them and for God to open a door of opportunity to minister to them. We are to pray for laborers who will be available to them. If we have loved ones in another city or state, we can pray God will send laborers into their path. I pray that for some I know, and am also praying for those who will disciple new believers. I ask Him to send on-fire, Holy Ghost-filled, Bible-believing, Word-talking, faith-speaking believers into their lives. I don't want some religious person coming to say to them, "Oh, you're okay." I need someone to go to them and say, "Hey, if you'll just believe the Word and do what the Bible says, if you'll just start believing and walking with God according to the Scriptures, God will save you and start blessing your life." That's the kind of person we need to pray God will send to our unbelieving, or backsliding, lost family members. They need someone with an anointing of the Holy Ghost and discerning of spirits to discern the situation, who will not be fooled or deceived by their words, and who will speak the power of the Word into their lives.

GOD EXPECTS BELIEVERS TO PARTICIPATE IN THE HARVEST

Jesus prayed some very powerful words in His High Priestly prayer noted in John 17:18. I've been studying the 17th chapter of John for several months, and I've made nugget notes from the Lord. I'm going to preach a series from them one of these days. ***"As You sent Me into the world, I also have sent them into the world." (John 17:18***

Does that sound like we have a choice in this? No, we are to participate in the harvest, period. We are to gather the lost into the kingdom of God. It is time to get bold and talk to our in-laws, our parents, brothers and sisters, our neighbors and co-workers. "You know I love you, and you may not like what I'm going to tell you right now. There is only one thing I can give you which can give you hope for the future. It is Jesus! He is the One I have found." We must be bold if we are to participate in the harvest.

I want you to see this. Jesus said, "as" the Father sent Him. This is a very interesting word. Jesus sends us just as He was sent by the Father. How many of us understand according to this Scripture that Jesus was sent with power? He was not sent powerless. He was not sent without the anointing of the Holy Spirit. The Bible says in ***Acts 10:38, "how God anointed Jesus of Nazareth with the Holy Spirit and with power, who went about doing good and healing all who were oppressed by the devil, for God was with Him."*** And Jesus said, "Father, as You sent Me -- as You were with Me -- I am sending them. I am not sending them without power, because the same power You gave to Me, I gave to them."

As Jesus was sent, we are sent. We are not sent out without equipment! We are sent out with the power of the Holy Spirit in us. We have the Word of God, which is the sword of the Spirit, and we can conquer any demonic force trying to stop us from winning our family and friends to Jesus! We have the same authority Jesus had! Hallelujah! He said "as" I was sent, I am sending you. We are sent in the same power as Jesus!

"Jesus said to them, 'Peace to you. As the Father has sent Me, I also send you.'" (John 20:21-22)

The first thing Jesus tells us in this verse is, "Peace to you." Don't get upset, stressed out, don't get worried, but be at peace. As God sent Him, He sends us. Jesus didn't come into this world intimidated by the devil. He didn't come into this world afraid what the Pharisees were going to say to, or about Him. He didn't come afraid of what religious spirits would try to do to Him. He didn't come fearing what Pilate would do. He didn't come afraid of the Cross. Jesus came in the power and anointing of the Father with the glory of God in His life and peace in His heart. That is why He could stand up in a ship in the middle of a storm and say, "Peace be still," because He is peace. He gives us power and anointing right along with peace. Jesus is speaking to us today, "As the Father sent Me I send you in the power of the same Spirit."

"You shall receive power after the Holy Spirit is come upon you, and you shall be witnesses." (Acts 1:8)

Do you see there is no choice in this matter? When we get the power of the Holy Spirit upon, in, and flowing through us, there is going to be a witness which causes people to look at us and say, "What's up with you? What's different about you?"

I walked into an office the other day and you could cut the atmosphere with a knife it was so thick with tension. I wore a smile when I entered to talk to a friend. I looked him in the eye as I greeted him. I told him God wanted me to drop off something for him. It happened to be a box of candy. Yes, it was for a man, a businessman! The Lord told me to take him some sweets and let him know I care about his life. You thought we only gave chocolates to our wives, didn't you?

When I handed it to him, a big smile came on his face, even though before that his look was like him saying, "You don't know the pressure I'm under today!" That simple act did something for this guy who doesn't know Jesus. He's really close to accepting the Lord, and I want to be the one who gets to lead him to Jesus! I've built a two-year relationship with this man, and he's so close to having his life radically changed. He'll never be the same, and everything he puts his hands to will never be the same either. Are you catching the heart of the Spirit here?

GOD EXPECTS BELIEVERS TO PRESERVE THE HARVEST

We pray the harvest in, we participate in it, and then we are to preserve the harvest. In other words, we retain it, keep it, nurture it, and disciple it. Do you know how we do that? With compassion! We must keep our focus on remembering if it weren't for Jesus, we wouldn't be where we are today. We wouldn't be at our level of maturity if it weren't for Jesus. I realize that level is different for everyone, but if not for Jesus, we wouldn't be enjoying any level of blessings, and we wouldn't have peace or joy either. Perhaps we might experience a measure of temporal happiness, but we wouldn't have eternal joy residing on the inside. We keep all that in focus when we participate in preserving the harvest. We will do so with compassion, love, and acceptance of right where that person is at in that moment of time.

New people may come to us dressed differently, either worse or better. Hey, I know human nature! If someone is dressed much better than we are, will we have the attitude, "Man, who do they think they are?" Or if someone else arrives dressed worse, will we think to ourselves, "Wow, look at them!" Folks, that is not love! Those types of attitudes will not produce or retain a harvest.

What preserves the harvest is compassion for people. What will happen if some Sunday we find someone new sitting in "our pew?" (because we were late). If we get upset about it, we better run to the altar that day and get saved. I'm as serious as I can be. Hey, you can sit in my spot. I'll just move and sit somewhere else. I'm serious. I'll move to a far corner if someone wants to sit on the front row and worship God.

We might find one day someone not quite as "polished" as we are, not as wealthy or affluent as we are, or perhaps they are downright poor or uneducated. What we need to focus on is, they are lost! They need Jesus! Jesus loves one and all. Let's love and accept all of them with compassion, then go greet, minister, and care for them.

Compassion is a divine force of love that desires to help. "Let me help you. I see you're new today here. Is there anything I can pray with you about this week?" That kind of caring is not just for the ushers and greeters, it is for all of us. "I just noticed the Lord really moved on you in the service today. May I just pray with you? Tell me what God is doing in your life and let's just agree together in prayer. Let me give you my phone number. Call me if you have any needs or if you need prayer. Call me anytime of the day or night." Are you hearing this? That is what compassion in action looks and sounds like.

If someone shares a need with us, don't run to the pastor, "Pastor, come over here, this person needs prayer." No, you pray for them. I'm not God. God desires to use all of us in the Body of Christ. He wants to flow through all of our hands, hearts, spirits, amen? There is a powerful principle and anointing here even though I'm ribbing you about all of this.

Compassion flows from the deepest part of our being. Compassion releases an anointing from God. Compassion is God's character revealed. Compassion is motivated by love.

"And on some have compassion, making a difference. But others save with fear, pulling them out of the fire, hating even the garment defiled by the flesh." (Jude 22)

God is gathering a harvest and is inviting us to join with Him in it. Our responsibility is to pray for it, to participate in it, and to preserve the harvest, so the kingdom of God can advance and be blessed. Each of us is a part. Each time I give an altar call and people come forward to accept Jesus, every one of us is a part of the reaping, because we've prayed for the harvest and we've brought them with us to the house of God.

God expects us to stand strong in spirit, He expects us to be ready to give an answer for the hope that lies within us, and He expects us to gather in His harvest. We don't have to be great mathematicians to figure this out, but if every one of us brought someone with us to the house of the Lord, we would double attendance. That would provide many more people given opportunity to come to Jesus. Wouldn't that be awesome?

The Holy Spirit is calling some people to Himself right now. The Spirit of God is speaking to lives. I know many of you are already at a place in your spiritual life where you know you have eternal life, but there are others who are still on the way to finding Jesus. I speak to you today. May I have the privilege of leading you to Jesus as your Lord and Savior?

The Bible says all we have to do is believe in our heart and confess with our mouth the Lord Jesus, and we will be saved. That's it. He will bring us out of despair, struggles, and bring us to Himself and give us His life. He forgives us of the past, and I mean anything or everything we've ever done in our life. He leaves it behind and starts us on a fresh new path with Him. If you've never received Jesus as your Savior, or if you are in the process of finding him, today is your opportunity to respond to Him. Perhaps you have once known the Lord but now you want to come back to Him. I want to pray for you.

One, you've reached the crossroads of making the greatest decision of your life. Don't let the devil talk you out of it.

Realize God is voting for you. This is a victory decision. When you make the choice, you come to Jesus.

Next, go ahead and turn your life over to Him. It is a bold step, but you are telling the devil, "I'm leaving you behind and I going over to Jesus right now."

Heavenly Father, thank You for Jesus who gives me peace, life, and contentment, and who forgives me all of my sins. I ask You to forgive me today, and come into my life. Be the Lord of my life from this day forward. I give myself to You, in Jesus' mighty Name. Thank You, Lord, amen.

Hallelujah, Jesus! Lift your hands to the Lord as I close this chapter with prayer.

Father, You have stirred up our spirit. We will not only pray for the harvest, we will participate in the gathering, and in preserving the harvest. I thank You, Father, for the anointing of God upon every person reading this, and in Jesus' mighty Name, I thank You, Father, that You are already using us, and will use us to an even greater measure to bring the lost to You. Thank You, Lord, for empowering us to do it. In Jesus' mighty Name, amen.

Now go, bless someone and lead them to Jesus!

Chapter Two

Filled with the Holy Spirit

"For God so loved the world [the world represents those without Jesus], ***that He gave His only begotten Son, that whoever believes in Him should not perish but have everlasting life. For God did not send His Son into the world to condemn the world but that the world through Jesus might be saved." (John 3:16-17)***

This is God's season. God's season is opposite from the world's season. Every week we see and hear in the media of new developments in our world regarding the future of America and the other nations of the world. We are hearing rapidly unfolding new developments on a daily basis. As believers we do not focus on the news but rather upon God's promised season when He will perform miraculous and powerful signs and wonders in the earth.

Let's pray before we begin this chapter:
Father, in the mighty Name of Jesus I thank You for the anointing of God for this subject. Jesus is with us. We sense Your presence, Lord, and there's a joy,

excitement, and enthusiasm in our hearts, and we will not lose this enthusiasm when we finish this chapter. I thank You we will walk with our head held high, our shoulders back, a smile on our face, and joy of the Lord in our heart. The Word of God working mightily in and through us, with the Name of Jesus stamped upon us, the anointing of God surrounding us, the angels of the Lord walking with us, and the power of the Word working within us, both to will and do Your good pleasure. I thank You, Father, and I give You praise in Your wonderful and awesome Name, amen.

We already know the Bible declares where sin abounds, the Word of God, the grace and ability of God helping us do what we cannot do for ourselves, abounds still more (Romans 5:20). All of us have seen horrible tragedies in the news of people being trampled, others being burned in fires, pictures of beheadings, as well as many other tragedies which brought destruction to hundreds of lives. I'm not going to try to pursue the answer to whether tragedies are God's judgment for sin. Tragedies are heart-rending, but I do not know if they happen as a result of sin. I simply know there is a law of sowing and reaping at work in the world as well as in our individual lives.

I do know with a certainty, however, this is a season of time where God is calling people to Himself. It is strong in my spirit that too many times we wait until tragedy occurs before we begin to pray, hoping we can somehow change the outcome. Prayer will not change the outcome once the tragedy happened. The only change which happens after the fact is the change which can happen inside those who pray. God doesn't want us to wait until crisis happens before we run to Him in prayer.

I am excited to be alive in this season where God is doing incredible things! It is my firm belief we are going to hear good reports about what believers have been praying for aired in the news one of these days. Instead of hearing about all the bad stuff we are going to hear, "Revival breaks out in Billings, MT!" We are going to hear, "Children at the church hit the streets witnessing to people and bringing them to Jesus!" I'm not saying that just to make us feel good.

I really believe a day is coming soon when we will hear those kinds of good news reports. "A lady gets out of a wheelchair and walks the aisles of a local church!" Or, "Man arrives at church blind but walks out with new eyes!" Or, "A deaf lady arrives in local church and receives instant healing for ears and speech." I hope this is getting into our spirits! We are living in God's season of the miraculous, hallelujah!

It is difficult not to view or listen to all the negative reports in the news today, but God wants us to instead focus our attention on what He is doing around the world.

The promise of Joel 2:28-29 is still the same. The Lord said, ***"I will pour out My Spirit upon all flesh in those days."*** Speak that aloud with conviction, "God said I will pour out My Spirit on all flesh in those days." The "those days" spoken about here are these days! These are the days the prophet Joel was talking about. These are those days prophesied by Joel. He wasn't referring to the Day of Pentecost when the Spirit of God was poured out. Because of the Acts 2 Pentecost event, the Holy Spirit of God is still being poured out in our day. We are living in that season. The day and times we are living in right now are "those days."

In the middle of this season for His harvest of blessings, salvation of souls, end-time revival, and of pouring out His Spirit, God has an expectation of every believer. I'll give some definitions before we proceed.

"Expect" means a sense of watching or intense anticipation. Are we watching with intense anticipation for what God wants to do in these days? I was meditating on this recently. The Scripture says the Lord is going to pour out His Spirit upon all flesh. His expectation for this day, His watching of this day, His intense anticipation of this day, is for the great harvest which will come into the kingdom of God because He is pouring out the Holy Spirit even in the middle of all the unrest and uncertainty in our world these days. I sense this so strong from the heart of the Father! He knows what is going on in the earth, but He also knows what He has planned for this season of time. Millions, perhaps billions, of people the world over will come to a saving knowledge and personal relationship with Jesus Christ!

Can you imagine the joy of the Father on the throne in heaven with Jesus, His Son, at His right hand? The

Bible says Jesus is making intercession for us. The Father's joy is great because He sent the Holy Spirit upon the earth to work and to gather in the great harvest of souls. People will come to know and love Jesus and escape the fires of hell in this season in which we live! Can you imagine the joy of the Father? Our God is right now loosing His anointing upon people everywhere who will tell others about the joy they've found, and bring them to Jesus Christ. You know that puts a smile on my face too!

I sat across the table from a couple of young men recently. One recently gave his life to Jesus. The other is still in the process of finding Jesus, (and I'm going to help him do it). As we sat visiting, I sensed a little resistance, a little pride, a little machoism in him, yet deep down inside my heart I'm smiling to myself because of the anticipation I have telling me it won't be long now before this fellow gives his life to Jesus. It doesn't look that way in the natural right now as he walks through some struggles and hassles in his life. But as I sat there, I had to be careful not to laugh out loud because of my joy and anticipation stirring on the inside. I didn't want to laugh in his face, but I sat there with a joy inside of me and a knowing in my spirit, that it will not be very long before that young man admits his need for Jesus. I am also anticipating the opportunity to tell him, "Jesus is where your help comes from. Look to Jesus, the Author and Finisher of faith." I was already looking forward to saying, "He is present with us right now and desires to radically bless and change your life!"

We are privileged to live in this season of time! It is God's season! He, too, is anticipating the results of His pouring out of the Holy Spirit. He is anticipating the great miracles He will show upon the earth. He is anticipating the blind seeing, the deaf hearing, and the lame walking. He is anticipating cancer tumors disappearing from people's bodies. He is anticipating whole families coming to the altar and giving themselves to Jesus. He has an expectation and anticipation for us to co-partner with Him for these results. He has an expectation of us to fulfill our part in bringing about what He is desiring to do in this season.

There were probably more than 400+ people gathered in our Community Life Center gymnasium recently for our basketball awards ceremony. Basketball is one of our outreach ministries into our city. These 400 heard the Gospel preached to them at the awards ceremony. Some of them received Jesus for the first time, while others rededicated their lives to Christ. The Gospel was preached, and the love of Jesus was released in the gymnasium. I wish you could have been there to see what happened. It was awesome! The Spirit of the Lord was present in the gym. I had people come to me afterwards remarking, "Wow! That was incredible. There are no other sports leagues in this city doing anything like that!" I said, "You're absolutely right. This league focuses on Jesus in order to bring people to Him."

God's anticipation of these events is His desire to pull in the net, draw the harvest in from any direction He can, from any arena of life He can, including sports.

Our Community Life Center sports program and gymnasium are but the vehicle for Him to use to draw in His harvest. That is what makes this season of time so exciting! You and I get to be a part of bringing people to a personal relationship with Jesus. That thrills me! It can happen anywhere, even when we are at work, in the grocery store, on the school campus, in a professional building, in a doctor's office. The dental office is my personal favorite. They call it dentistry, I call it ministry!

WHAT ARE BELIEVERS TO BE?

God has an expectation of harvest and wants to use us to bring someone to Christ. We represent God in the earth. We are not our own representative, but God's. I do not pastor The Gail Craig Church. This is not my church. It is God's Church. We are all operating on that level in relationship to what God wants to do in using us. His expectation is the same for all believers. We are to go to the "highways" and compel them to come in, so that His house may be full. He is not just talking about this house, the physical church, but the heavenly home for believers in Christ as Lord. His expectation is for us to be His representative.

WHAT ARE BELIEVERS TO DO?

God is anticipating awesome and incredible things to take place. He has expectations of His children. Say with me, "I am His Child! I belong to Jesus!" For instance, I understand my relationship with my two children and how I would do anything, I mean anything, for them, in sacrifice, or to bless their lives. I know my Heavenly Father has that same kind of attitude toward me, as His child, and just as I have expectations of my children to grow, to obey, and to mature, God has these same expectations of His children.

Why does God expect the same things from us, His children? Because we have been purchased with the Blood of Christ, His firstborn. We do not own ourselves, and we don't belong to ourselves. The Father purchased us with the precious Blood of His own beloved son, Jesus. Do we truly understand that? Paul said we are not our own anymore. We belong to the King of the universe, and the King has expectations of our life. He wants to fulfill His expectations for our life, because we've been purchased and adopted as sons and heirs, saved from the wrath to come, and sent out into the world to bring others to Jesus. God expects this response from us in this season.

In the last chapter we talked about standing strong in Spirit in this day, to be ready to give an answer for the hope inside of us. We are to be ready to give an answer why we are so happy. We are to be ready to give an answer for our joy and peace in the midst of tumult. We are to be ready to give an answer why the events and circumstances in our lives don't get us down and depressed. The last chapter also dealt with gathering in God's harvest; God expects us to pray for it, participate in it, and to preserve the harvest. In this chapter I want to talk to you about another point:

GOD EXPECTS BELIEVERS TO BE FILLED WITH THE HOLY SPIRIT

God expects us to be filled and overflowing with the Holy Spirit. There are many necessary and unnecessary activities which fill our lives. We can fill every hour in our day with something if we want to, and most of us do. We're filling it with eating, sleeping, working, and other things. It's not hard to fill our day. Yet, in this day, in this season we live in God expects believers, in this season of His miracle working power, to be filled with the Holy Spirit.

"Therefore, do not be unwise but understand what the will of the Lord is." (Ephesians 5:17)

The original Greek word used for "unwise" in this passage really means stupid and making dumb decisions. There is something very important to me and my life, and that is to fulfill God's will. I don't ever want to be caught in the permissive will of God, or hear Him say, "Well, I guess I can let you do that for a little while if that is what you choose." I would rather live in the perfect will of God, where I know beyond doubt I am walking in the will and blessing of the Lord. Are you with me on that one? I don't want to walk in His permissive will. He doesn't actually give us permission to walk in His permissive will, but we think we can get forgiveness easier if we ask for permission first. What that really means is we intend to do our own thing for a while and hope it is okay with God, with the intention of asking His forgiveness later.

I would rather walk in a place of blessing with God where I know I am doing what God wants me to do, and I know I am becoming who God wants me to be, and I know I'm walking and living how He wants me to walk and live. That way I never have to worry about, stress about, or wonder if I will get an answer when I pray, because I am living right in the center of God's will for my life.

Our Ephesians Scripture infers God wants us to understand His will. "The will of the Lord" is defined in the original text as the determined plan of God, His inclination, His pleasure, His purpose. The will of God has to do with specific things for our life. Look at that verse again, using today's vernacular, ***"Do not be unwise, stupid or make bad choices, but understand what the determined plan of the Lord is for our life."***

In God's divine provision, He determined beforehand we would need His power to live, His anointing to operate, and His wisdom to serve Him in this season. He gives His Holy Spirit to live inside every born-again child of God for that purpose. He gives His Holy Spirit to empower and to abide inside every believer. He knew beforehand this season in time was coming. He prophesied it in the Word of God as He moved upon holy men of God.

God is not unaware or surprised about any of the events happening in our world right now. He made provision for, set in His divine order, that in this season we would need the power of the Holy Spirit in and for our life, not just around us, but inside of us. He knew we would need His anointing, not just surrounding us when we come together in church, but literally dwelling in, living in, abiding in the inner man of every born-again believer. No matter what happens in the natural, the power of the Holy Spirit will work in those within whom He dwells, and He will empower them in the middle of this season and time.

"Do not be drunk with wine in which is dissipation." (Ephesians 5:18)

Let me explain the background of the Church of Ephesus. The people received Christ but kept on doing what the world did. They did not separate themselves from the things of the world. Paul's challenge to them was to be continually filled with the Holy Spirit, not a counterfeit of "spirits," which try to control one's life and debilitate them, but to allow the Holy Spirit to work in their life. "Dissipation" in another Bible translation means debauchery of any kind. Now let's go back to that same verse:

". . .but be filled with the Spirit."

God's determined will and purpose for every single person born again by the Blood of Jesus is to be filled with the Holy Spirit. God's expectation is for us to have an experience with Him, an encounter with Him, and to be so filled with the Holy Spirit that He can be seen in our life. I'll tell you in a moment what that evidence is. God's determination in this day is that you and I are filled with the Holy Spirit, not with a counterfeit, not with themselves, not with our own agendas, not with our own thinking, feelings, or philosophies about life.

His determined purpose for this season in time is for us to be filled to overflowing with the Holy Spirit. That is why He said in Joel, chapter two, ***"in those days,"*** which are these days, ***"I am going to pour out My Spirit on all flesh."*** God said, "I'm pouring it out!" Say aloud, please, "The Holy Spirit is being poured out upon me!" Hallelujah! In that pouring out God wants us to be filled, filled, filled with the Holy Spirit, which is the anointing of our God. He is doing the filling. He is the new wine of heaven. He is the ever-flowing fountain. He is the sweet refreshing.

The Promise of the Holy Spirit is for Everyone. ***"For the promise is for you, to your children, to all who are afar off, and as many as the Lord our God will call." (Acts 2:39)***

The "promise" of the Holy Spirit which is spoken here is announcing a divine assurance of good. God's intention is not that we will barely squeak by in this season, or for us to just make it by the skin of our teeth. I don't have any skin on my teeth so that should tell us it's really tough to make it that way, right? That is a worldly attitude, and even at times within Christianity, "I just need enough to get by." "I just need enough of Jesus to squeak me by today and maybe I'll come back again next week for a little bit more. Maybe I won't need any more." That's the world's way of thinking, but not God's anticipation. His anticipation is to fill us to overflowing with the

Holy Ghost every day. He wants us to come to Him daily for a fresh outpouring of His Spirit. He wants to put His anointing on us every day because He knows what we face in the world. He knows our need for His anointing. God knows why we need to be filled with the power of God.

I'm not talking about a little Holy Ghost goose bump feeling so we can say, "Oooohh, wasn't that nice?" When we go out and fight the real war with the devil, we're not going to be able to think, "Oooohh, hey, that's cool!" and defeat Satan, unless we have God's power inside. Don't get me wrong. I'm not against feeling the presence of God. I love the feeling of being in the anointing of God. I love the presence of the Holy Spirit, but I love Him more on the inside than on the outside. I know when He is on the inside of me He will stir up what I need and then release it in victory on the outside. That is a good place to shout hallelujah to the Lord!

THE EVIDENCE OF BEING FILLED WITH THE HOLY SPIRIT IS SPEAKING IN OTHER TONGUES

You knew the "T" word was coming, didn't you? I'll tell you, the T word is one of the most powerful words I know, because the Bible says when I pray in the Spirit, I'm talking directly to God! My spirit is praying things I may not be aware of at that moment, but I will get the understanding later. When I'm praying in tongues I know God is helping or preparing me for what is ahead, because the Spirit prays according to the will of God. Speaking in tongues is not something to be afraid of! Speaking in tongues is a connection between the Father and me. It is our heavenly prayer language in which we magnify God and touch His heart.

I was talking with one of my son's one day. He was nine years old at the time. He was telling me about something that happened in his life after he was baptized in water. He was at school the following day, and had some thoughts hurled at him which he knew were not right. I instructed him, "Drew, when the enemy brings thoughts or lies against you urging you to do something you know is not right, that is the perfect time to pray in your heavenly language. Pray in tongues, Son."

Some may say the baptism in the Holy Spirit is not real, but at age nine my son knew it was real! We can counter-attack any spiritual attack by praying in the Spirit, because when we magnify God in tongues we send the enemy to flight. There is no room for our thoughts or imagination, because we are praying a perfect prayer to the Father, in Jesus' Name, by the anointing of God.

What God expects of believers in this day is to be filled with the Holy Spirit, not to have a one-time experience where we spoke in tongues 25 years ago. Each day we are to minister to the Lord in our beautiful heavenly prayer language. As we do, we are magnifying and blessing Him, and at the same time He infuses us with His power when we don't know what to do on our own. He drives the enemy away from us, so he can never come back in that particular area of our life again, because now the Holy Spirit has taken up residence there. There is no room for the devil to occupy there because the Holy Spirit now occupies and continues to dwell in that area of our life. The enemy can no longer control us there because Jesus has taken the territory back to Himself, filled, and empowered us as we prayed in tongues. Isn't that reason alone enough to desire the baptism of the Holy Spirit and tongues? I love teaching about the Holy Spirit!

We can follow through the Book of Acts and see examples of tongues as the evidence of being filled with the Holy Spirit. Every time someone received the Holy Spirit, they spoke with other tongues:

". . . spoke with other tongues as the Spirit gave utterance." (Acts 2:9)

"They heard them speak with tongues the wonderful works of God." (Acts 2:11)

". . . heard them speak with tongues and magnify God . . ." (Acts 10:46)

". . . Holy Spirit came upon them and they spoke with tongues and prophesied." (Acts 19:6)

Speaking in tongues is the initial, physical evidence of the baptism of the Holy Spirit. Let me tell you something about tongues. It brings a powerful relationship with God! Tongues produce an awesome and intimate relationship with the Lord.

REASONS WHY GOD EXPECTS US TO BE FILLED WITH THE HOLY SPIRIT

1. The Holy Spirit Enables Us to Live an Overcoming Life.

We're only human beings -- human -- with a carnal nature needing to be dealt with all the time. Our carnal, human, soulish nature wants to control our lives due to original sin in the Garden of Eden. We all must deal with that nature originating in our soul man. God's expectation for us being filled with the Holy Spirit is so we can live an overcoming life in His Spirit rather than muddling through life from our carnal nature. In other words, He gives us personal power through the indwelling Holy Spirit. His power helps us through life! I want you to see something very powerful. It may seem backwards to us, but the Greek is at times inverted:

"See then that you walk circumspectly, not as fools, but as wise, redeeming the time because the days are evil." (Ephesians 5:15-16)

This verse tells us why we need to be filled with the Spirit. Here we see that word, "fools," again. "Circumspectly" is an interesting word as well. "Circumspectly" in Greek means to be most exact or straight, purposeful, and accurate. This verse instructs us to walk straight and purposely in our walk with the Lord. We are not to get off the path and miss out on what God is doing in these days, or be on a parallel path. He wants us to be so filled with the Holy Spirit as to be constantly tuned into Him. Then we will not miss the miracles God wants to pour into and through us. We won't miss the debt cancellation He has for us. We won't miss our healing, salvation for our loved ones and family, or miss the opportunities God brings to us. God wants us to walk purposefully and accurately, not behaving stupidly, not being misled, not being a simpleton or unwise. He wants us to be filled with the Holy Spirit, so we walk in His Wisdom.

"Redeem the time" is powerful, and means to rescue from loss. In other words, "don't lose out." It also means to improve opportunity. We are to be filled with the Holy Spirit, so we can walk the path He has for us in the Spirit, not give in to sin, but overcome the enemy in every part of our life and improve our opportunity in God. We are empowered to take advantage of every opportunity He gives us to touch the lives of other people. When He says we are to redeem the time, He means we are to be aware of the season in which we live so He can bring opportunities to us. If we are not filled with His power or listening for His wisdom, we will miss these opportunities.

If the economy of this world should crash, God will tell us how to be blessed. He will tell us where to put our money. I already know where that is. He says to lay up treasure in heaven where a thief cannot break in and steal. God will give us wisdom and opportunity, both for our own personal victories, but also to bring others into the kingdom of God. Everything God does in our life is not just to bless us, but to bring others to Christ.

God has a dual purpose for blessing us which always includes those whom He brings to us, those we are in contact with, so we will explain why we are happy and at peace during these troubled times. "I am happy and at peace because Jesus is moving in my life, and you can have the same blessings of God that I walk in, if you will receive Jesus as your Lord and Savior."

It's true! We are to be filled with the Holy Spirit, so we can live an overcoming life and utilize every opportunity to redeem the time during this season of God's timing. The Holy Spirit keeps us in tune with God. We need Him on the inside, so He can flow to the outside. The Holy Spirit will repair on the inside that which needs work, so we can walk circumspectly on the outside.

I bought a pair of shoes on sale at a certain store in town. I wore the shoes about four weeks and they fell apart. Right on the ball of my foot all the stitching fell out and the leather came apart. It looked like I had a little mouth on the side of my shoe. I knew this to be a reputable store, so I thought I would return the shoes or exchange them for a new pair. I wore them to the store, put them on the counter, and the clerk confirmed the store would happily exchange the shoes. I liked these shoes, they were nice, and I was glad I could get a new pair. I put them on and walked out.

About four weeks later they blew out again in the same way. I again returned to the store, pulled off my shoe, and placed it on the counter. I explained to the clerk I had already exchanged them, but now the other shoe fell apart the same way. The lady looked at the shoe then asked me, "Are you wearing this shoe outside?" (I thought the same thing you just thought, but I told myself to bite my tongue.)

She went on to explain this particular type of shoe is an indoor shoe. I'm thinking to myself, "This is so hilarious!" At our house we take our shoes off when we come indoors, and I'm thinking to myself, "She wants me to wear them inside but take them off when I go outside!" I bit my tongue because I was thinking, "The reason I wear shoes is so I can go outside and not hurt my feet!" I am biting my lip by this time, wondering how to reply to the clerk. Finally, I asked if she could just give me a gift card in exchange for the "indoor" shoes. She said surely, but she continued to be stuck on the fact the shoes should not be worn outside. She proceeded to try to sell me some vinyl shoe covers to pull over the indoor shoes when I go outside, but I declined. She did give me a gift card, perhaps because I didn't argue with her about whether it was an indoor or an outdoor shoe.

The Holy Spirit nudged me by bringing this thought: "Sometimes people treat the Holy Spirit just like that! They don't want Me to work on the inside." It's okay if He gives us goose bumps on the outside by shining on us a little bit. But do we really want Him to work on the inside, because that might mean we may have to change.

You know what? What God expects of us in this day and age is to be so filled with the Spirit that the inside changes and the outside is aglow with the glory of God, and other people can't help but noticing! That's the kind of "shoe" we can wear anywhere! We could bathe in them if we wanted to. No matter what our personal weather, it cannot diminish what God, by His Spirit, is doing inside of us.

When it comes to the Holy Spirit, God expects believers and His church to be filled with His Spirit. If we are, I'll guarantee the Spirit in us will draw people to Jesus. People are looking for reality. They are tired of the same ole, same ole, same old thing. It's like an infomercial on TV. We get tired of hearing the same old, same old thing, over and over. They repeat their spiel over and over because they know if we hear it enough, we'll just go out and buy it.

People are looking for the reality of God, and they desire to have His anointing. They are hungering for more than what they've had. We have people sitting in our church who have said to me personally, "I've got to have more of God! I've got to go to a higher level with Him, because I sense God wants to take me deeper." That may be why you are reading this right now. You could be anywhere else, but you are reading this in the presence of God because you realize the season in which we live. It is a season in God's timing to be filled with the Holy Spirit's power. It is time to let Him flow through our life, so we can live as overcomers and be witnesses of His overcoming power and reality in this season.

2. The Holy Spirit Enables Us to Overcome Lusts.

"Walk in the Spirit and you shall not fulfill the lusts of the flesh." (Galatians 5:16)

There are many types of lust, and each of us has trouble with one kind or another. With some it is lust for drugs, alcohol, pleasure, shopping, eating, and the list goes on and on. How do we walk circumspectly as overcomers over the lusts of the flesh if we are not filled with the Spirit of God? We are empowered from on high to live in, dwell in, and be filled with the power and anointing of the Spirit of God, and as we walk by faith in His Spirit, He speaks, "This is the way, walk in it, My child." The Holy Spirit is faithful to tell us to turn here or go there, move a certain direction, do this or that, give this up, but He also gives us the power to be overcomers in any area we seek Him. To walk in the Spirit means we will not fulfil the lusts of our flesh.

3. The Holy Spirit Enables Us to Live in Liberty and Freedom.

God's expectation for believers is to be filled with the Spirit so we will experience freedom in every area of our life and to bring the news of this freedom to others. Let's look at this from God's perspective from His Word:

"Now the Lord is the Spirit [the Holy Spirit] and where the Spirit of the Lord is there is liberty." (II Corinthians 3:17)

The Holy Spirit is the manifestation of the Father and the Son in the earth and in our lives. God's expectation for us is to have liberty and freedom in Jesus, from guilt, shame, bondage, burdens, fear, from attacks of the devil, from oppression, deception of mind, and free from torment. The Holy Spirit brings these freedoms, purchased for us by the blood of Jesus! Say to yourself, "Smile and let some freedom out!" There is liberty!

"Stand fast in the liberty [Spirit] by which Christ has made us free and do not be entangled with the yoke of bondage." (Galatians 5:1)

Both "freedom" and "liberty" mean emancipation from bondage, exemption from liabilities, unencumbered. "Lord, I am free from this thing, I'm not encumbered anymore. I don't carry the weight of my sin or bondage anymore. I'm free!" If we desire freedom and liberty in any area of our life, we ask and receive it from the Holy Spirit. I'll tell you there is nothing like being free from burdens and sin, free from guilt and failure! God's expectation for all believers is for us to live free in Jesus Christ by being filled with the Holy Spirit, freed from burdens and stress!

4. The Holy Spirit Brings a Powerful Prayer Life.

We cannot afford to be "religious" in prayer in this day and season. We live in a desperate day and we need to be powerful in prayer. The Bible says if we are baptized in the Holy Spirit, we are powerful prayers. Ephesians 6:18a gives a description of two kinds of prayers, ***". . . praying with all prayer and supplication in the Spirit."*** Both kinds of prayer are necessary and powerful, and the Bible promises they will produce faith. Now look at this:

"Likewise, the Spirit also helps our weaknesses. For we do not know what we should pray for as we ought, but the Spirit Himself makes intercession for us with groanings which cannot be uttered. Now He who searches the hearts knows what the mind of Christ is because He makes intercession for the saints according to the will of God." (Romans 8:26-27)

How many of us know our weaknesses? I think most of us are aware of our own weaknesses. How many of us realize the Holy Spirit will empower us in our weaknesses? Christ Jesus makes intercession for us according to the determined purpose of God. The determined purpose is for us to be filled with the Holy Spirit and with that dimension actively operating within, so we will have a powerful prayer life that the devil cannot interpret, diminish, stop, or shut down.

We can go to our prayer closet and pray in our heavenly language, or pray corporately in the Body of Christ in this language, and the devil doesn't know what we are talking about, hallelujah! The Holy Spirit searches our hearts, knows the will of God for us, and the Spirit prays the will of the Lord for us at that very moment in each situation. The Holy Spirit then releases the power of the Spirit of the Lord Jesus to help us live an overcoming life, hallelujah!

God expects believers to be filled with the Spirit, every day. Lust will not be able to conquer, neither will fear. The devil may still try to get to us, but because we are filled with the Holy Spirit and the Word of God, he is powerless. The Holy Spirit brings the Word of God into remembrance to minister Truth, encourage us, build our faith, or to lift us up. The Holy Spirit uses the Word to provide whatever we need at that moment. Go ahead and tell Him thank you!

Lift your hands to the Lord as the anointing of the Holy Spirit fills our praises. The anointing of the Lord is present, and He wants to fill you with the Holy Spirit and give you a prayer language. "You mean, Pastor, I can receive right now?" "Yes, you can, right where you are if you will reach out to the Lord and begin to worship Him."

God expects His church -- believers -- to be filled with the Holy Spirit. His expectation is for signs, wonders, and miracles to follow us. This is the season for it. He expects prosperity, yes, even now in the middle of economic distress, because He is the One who provides all the blessing, favor, and all the necessary anointing for prosperity in every area of our life.

If you are hungry for the baptism of the Holy Spirit with the initial evidence of speaking in tongues, lift your hands to Jesus right now and tell Him, "Lord, I'm hungry for more of You. I want to be filled, not half full - I don't even want to be one pint low - I want to be filled to overflowing with the Holy Spirit of God. Jesus, fill me now with Your Holy Spirit, Your holy presence. I am hungering for this next step for my life. Holy Spirit, I want You, I need You; fill me, and give me my prayer language.

Father, I ask You to loose Your presence into every life, loose Your glory into every person, in the Name of Jesus, and baptize these in Your Holy Spirit with the initial evidence of speaking in tongues. Thank You, Lord God.

Stand in His awesome presence right now with your hands lifted in supplication to Him. I want to pray the Holy Spirit will fall on you throughout the rest of this day, that you will feel the presence of God upon you, and you will want to worship God in your heavenly language. You will recognize the Holy Spirit when the power of God starts bubbling up inside you, like a fountain. Open your mouth and begin to praise Him in your heavenly language.

"Father, in Jesus' mighty Name, Your Holy Spirit's anointing is present with us. We sense Your presence and power. Father, in Jesus' Name, I ask You to baptize each hungry, seeking person reading this today. Those believers who have never experienced You in this dimension before, I ask that today may be the time when they begin to speak in their heavenly language to magnify You. I ask You, Father, to flow through them in blessing. Empower them I pray in Jesus' mighty Name, hallelujah! Amen.

Let your tongue begin to magnify God. Allow whatever words, not English or your native tongue, to come. Let your heavenly language come up out of your spirit, then utter out loud whatever God gives you. These words will not make sense to you, but they are filling the courts of heaven with perfect prayer and petition. Be filled with the Spirit of God so you can live an overcoming life, be able to overcome lusts, and have a powerful prayer life. Thank You, Father!

Here is something very important. If you have not received your new language in these moments but you know God is doing something inside, just keep seeking after God anyway, because perhaps just before you fall asleep on your bed tonight God will release your prayer language. You might be in your automobile or in your own kitchen when the Holy Spirit bubbles up within you. It is His desire to answer your seeking heart with His fullness.

Father, in the Name of Jesus, bless this wonderful, joy-filled, Spirit-filled, Word-filled, faith-filled people of God. Lord, our confession today is we will walk in the anointing of the Spirit. We are filled with the Holy Spirit of God, and You are faithful to bring forth the prayer language in every hungry person's life. I thank You for that today in Jesus' Name. Amen and amen!

Chapter Three

A Witness for Christ

"For I have come down from heaven, not to do My own will but the will of Him who sent Me. This is the will of the Father who sent Me, that of all He has given Me, I should lose nothing, but should raise it up at the last day. And this is the will of Him who sent Me, that everyone who sees the Son and believes in Him may have ever-lasting life, and I will raise him up at the last day." (John 6:38-40)

These are Jesus' own words, the red-letter text in our Bibles. Jesus came from heaven to do the will of His Father. Say this aloud, "The will of God for everyone who believes in Christ is to have everlasting life." There is no doubt that statement reflects the will and determined purpose of God.

We are living in a season of God's favor, anointing, release, provision and increase, and in His promised season of pouring out His Spirit on all flesh. It is His divine intent, His determined purpose, His plan, for this season in time. Aren't you glad you are alive to see it? God planned from ages past for the power of God to be released in this season, because He knew how much we would need the power of the Holy Spirit operating in our lives.

I have found this out personally. I realize I need the power of God more now than I ever thought I needed Him before. I firmly believe all Christians need the Holy Spirit's power more now than ever, because of the increase in intensity of Satanic operation in the earth. The Bible forewarned of this, but also assured us the Spirit of the Lord would also increase in the earth, and the power of God would be released in greater measure to His church. Every born-again believer who has received Jesus Christ is noticing this sin increase, but also noticing the Father's release of increased power and anointing of the Holy Spirit in our day.

Jesus said some very powerful things in the above Scripture. He did not come to earth to do His own will. This isn't a day for us to live by our own agendas. This is not the season to live according to our wants and desires. It is a season to live according to what God wants, and to participate with Him in what He desires to do. If we develop an attitude governed by our own wants and desires, we will miss the dynamic things which God is doing in this season, because our focus will not be upon the things of God but simply upon our own situations and circumstances. Our focus should not be about our will, but upon the will of God. Jesus came to do the Father's will.

Say aloud, "I am also sent to do My Father's will." Jesus repeats these same words twice, and then for a third time. He repeats Himself three times to reinforce the will of God became the will of the Lord.

In that will of God He said He would lose nothing. This is a season where the enemy is trying to come against people's lives, but the good news is this: we are not in a season of losing, hallelujah! We are in a season of winning! Jesus said that in this season, because He was doing the will of the Father, He would lose nothing.

WE LIVE IN A WINNING SEASON.

Let's look at the will of God, which means the determined plan of God. The determined plan of God for this season is for us to live in victory. Say aloud into the atmosphere, "I am not a loser! I am a winner in Christ Jesus!" God doesn't want us to lose one thing of what we possess. He doesn't want us to lose our family to the devil, or lose our own lives to the devil.

The only place in Scripture which mentions losing is when we come to Christ. When we give up our own life to take on His Life, we gain victory because we are putting on Jesus! That is the only reference connected to losing. Otherwise, it is a season of winning. We are not going to lose our spiritual battle, we cannot lose in this day and age in which we live. The Church (us) is not going to lose. We are winners in every situation according to the determined purpose of God. We win, Folks! Go ahead and shout about it!

The enemy will surely try his tactics against us, but we will not lose when we battle in the power of the Holy Spirit. I had this illustrated to me personally recently when the devil really tried to destroy me. Because the Bible tells me we don't lose in this season, I stood steadfast on that. Jesus said in the season of His determined plan I would not lose.

WE HAVE EVER LASTING LIFE

The second part of God's determined plan is everyone who believes in Jesus has everlasting life, and it is an overcoming life. In this season we don't lose since every promise God declared in His Word is ours. It may look in the natural we do not have, but according to the Word of God we do have. It may look like there is a wall up right now in the natural, but we have the victory already in the Name of Jesus! It is not the season of losing but the season of winning, a season of conquering, a season of overcoming.

God, therefore, has some great expectations of us. One, we are to stand strong in God in the Spirit. Two, we are to be ready to give an answer to those who ask. God expects us to tell others about the hope we have inside. Three, we are to be gathering the harvest by praying, participating, and preserving the harvest. Four, He expects us also to be filled with the Spirit for personal freedom and a powerful prayer life. The fifth point, the one we will study in this chapter, is God expects believers to be witnesses for Christ. Let's walk through some Scriptures to substantiate this point.

"But you shall receive power when the Holy Spirit has come upon you, and you shall be witnesses to Me in

Jerusalem, in all Judea and Samaria, and to the ends of the earth." (Acts 1:8)

Let me transliterate this Scripture for you from the original text, because the nuances of truth are powerful. "Power" in this Scripture is supernatural ability of God to do something for God. It is the supernatural ability, strength, and might of God doing the miraculous. This is quite separate from being born-again, or having power to be saved. The power referred to here has to do with miraculous power. These words are spoken by Jesus to His disciples. Jesus told them to go to the Upper Room and wait there for the Promise of the Father. He assured them His promise of the Spirit would surely come upon them there and they could then be witnesses for Him. In the Acts Scripture above, Jesus uses a different word for "power." He used the word *dunamis,* which means the supernatural might of God to perform miracles.

He said when we receive dunamis power it would transform us, change us, and do powerful things in our lives. There is a certain kind of power which comes into our lives when we are born-again. The Bible talks about that power as giving us the children's rights to the kingdom of God. That is why I want to lay a foundation to help you understand the difference in these two words, translated to our English word, "power."

"But as many as received Him [Jesus], to them He gave the power [in the original King James it is the word power, but the New King James uses the word right;

the Amplified Bible talks about privileges to become the children of God, even to those who believe on His Name." (John 1:12)

"Power" in this Scripture has to do with a power for privilege. It is not speaking here of dunamis power. This instance uses *exousia* in Greek, meaning right, authority, jurisdiction or privileges of the kingdom of God. When we receive Jesus as our Lord and Savior (born-again), He gives us the rights to the kingdom of God. We receive authority to operate in the Word, authority to pray, authority to receive the blessings of the kingdom of God.

The second power, however, *dunamis* power, means we receive power from the Holy Ghost to be witnesses. This power, or great anointing upon us, is to take us deeper into the nature and character of God. We have the right to become His children through privilege, but the dunamis power is supernatural ability coming in the Holy Spirit baptism to anoint us for greater works of service.

We can be born-again with the power and rights to the kingdom, but the anointing of the Holy Spirit provided by the baptism of the Spirit gives us the power to operate in the miraculous of God's kingdom. Are you with me on this?

The anointing from the baptism of the Holy Spirit releases power in believers for witnessing. The word "witness" is not the typical word that we would think. "Witness" means we must tell people about Jesus. We need to tell them about Jesus, we need to be talking to people about the victory they can have in Jesus. This word, "witness," when translated from the original text, comes from the word martyrs, or one who bears a record or gives testimony. This witness furnishes evidence or proof. The greatest proof of the power of God in our life is a transformed life. The greatest proof isn't that people get healed, or we have received a prayer language, but the greatest proof is that our lives are totally changed. The greatest proof is we are not bound to alcohol or drugs anymore, or to promiscuity or sex addictions anymore. That's the power of God which transforms us inwardly but produces outward, observable changes as well. Our lives become a testimony, or living proof of the transforming power of God. That is how this word witness is used here.

The proof of our transformation lies in the fact we are not what we used to be, we are who God says. We've been changed by His forgiveness and cleansing Blood, and given the rights to the kingdom of God. In the baptism of the Holy Spirit, we've been given the power to be totally transformed in every area of our life. The proof is we have passed from death into life, and we now live in the *Zoe* life of the Spirit of God, enabling us to listen to His voice and believe we are who He says we are, thus defeating the enemy's lies.

These proofs are visible to others. When someone looks at us, they know there is something different about us. "How come you don't do this anymore?" "Why don't you talk like this anymore?" Even our language is changed! Besides that, we aren't negative any longer. People can't help but wonder what happened to us. They are witnessing our transformation and it is the greatest witness we have to show to a lost world without Jesus. We don't need to go door-to-door hoping to win someone to Jesus, for we now have the greatest witness through our changed lives, and people notice and ask us questions! They want to know what is different because they like what they see. Say that aloud, "I'm different!" Yes, folks, we are a different bunch! Tell yourself, "I am proof that Jesus Christ is alive, and the power of the Holy Spirit is real!"

". . . and with great power the Apostles gave witness to the resurrection of the Lord Jesus. And great grace was upon them all." (Acts 4:33)

"Witness" here is the same word translated proof. "Great" means mega, so with mega dunamis they gave witness. In other words, the Apostles gave witness to the accounts of the supernatural ability of God, by the anointing of God. This is the might of God operating with great power. The Apostles performed great signs, wonders, and miracles. The crowds saw lame people walk, blind people see, deaf ears opened, and miracles of provision take place. With great power they gave witness, or proof to the resurrection of Jesus, and with great grace. Remember "grace" is the ability to help us do what we cannot do on our own. Great grace was upon them as they went about doing acts of power. Their witness, or the proof of God, was evidenced in their lives miraculously. How many of us want the proof of God in our lives miraculously?

". . . Behold I send the promise of My Father upon you but tarry in Jerusalem until you are endued with power from on high." (Luke 24:49)

"Endued" means to be clothed with, clothed in, or arrayed in. It's that same power for witness. Now picture this: God said we are endued with power. Say aloud, "I am clothed with the power of God through the baptism of the Holy Spirit, in order for me to give proof of the resurrection of Jesus, that He is alive in the world and in my life!" Hallelujah! We are clothed and filled with the power of God for a witness. In other words, we are to be a light in a dark place. Readers, I'm telling you the best is yet to come! This is getting "gooder and gooder!"

"You are the salt of the earth, but if the salt has lost its flavor, how shall it be seasoned? It is then good for nothing but to be thrown out and trampled underfoot by men. You are the light of the world. A city set on a hill cannot be hidden. Nor do they light a lamp and put it under a basket but on a lampstand, and it gives light to all that are in the house. Let your light so shine before men that they may see your good works and glorify your Father which is in heaven." (Matthew 5:13-16)

I want you to see something very powerful about this anointing upon our lives, this power to witness and to prove Jesus is alive. The Bible first of all calls us, "salt," and the translation means prudence. Believers keep balance in this world. We are the ones keeping the enemy from completely taking over this world.

Believers are those who hold the devil back by loosing the anointing of God. We are the salt of the earth for seasoning. In other words, we have His Spirit and power upon us in this season of God's expectation to be salt, and anointed with the power of God, so we can keep back the darkness of the enemy and loose the anointing of the Holy Spirit, allowing the light of God to shine forth. How many know we need salt in this season of seemingly bland things, gray areas, and scary happenings in the world?

We are "salty" believers anointed with the power of God's Spirit to give proof Jesus Christ is who He said He is, that He is the same yesterday, today and forever, and what He did then He is still doing now. We are anointed!

GOD EXPECTS BELIEVERS TO BE HIS WITNESSES

God provides all we need for witnessing. I want to share three things God gives to us which He expects us to use for Him:

1. Boldness.

The Bible calls the righteous, ***"bold lions,"*** and that ***"the wicked flee when no one is pursuing them" (Proverbs 28:1).*** Our boldness is a part of the proof showing that Jesus is alive. God gives us that boldness.

"And when they had prayed the place where they were assembled together was shaken and they were all filled

with the Holy Spirit and spoke the Word of God with boldness." (Acts 4:31)

"All were filled." Look what happened when the Spirit of the Lord filled their lives: they spoke the Word of God with boldness. In the original text, "boldness" means all were outspoken with assurance and confidence. Have you ever been in someone's presence who was so convinced they were right on a matter? You couldn't get them to back down because they were so convinced, assured, and confident about what they were speaking, and they weren't about to back away for anything. You know what? That is the way believers are supposed to be! We have opportunity every day to back away from the things of God. We face situations each day which could cause us to turn around and go the opposite direction.

I mentioned earlier in this chapter about being challenged by the enemy when he came against me so hard it was all I could think about. He was literally trying to destroy my thinking about whom I knew I was in Christ Jesus. I started making irrational decisions saying, "Well, I'm not going to do this then," or "What's the point of doing that then?" Come on, people, you've been there too!

The Holy Spirit stopped me. He said, "If you persist in thinking this way, you are giving in to the devil who has a plan to kill your faith." Have you ever had God spank you or slap you on one side of your head to get your attention? That's what effect He had on me. He told me, "Don't you dare step backwards from this situation, because if you do you are giving the devil a foothold." I told my wife I dared not back away. I had to face it, and I had to stir up some determination in my spirit. I prayed, "Okay, Lord, I will do as You've told me. I will walk into the den of the lions and I'm going to stand strong there expecting You to do what You said You would do." I mustered all the faith I possessed in my spirit to walk into the den of lions, and I wasn't about to be sorrowful, feel oppressed, or be doubtful in any way. "Lord, lift up my countenance when I don't feel like I can." Come on, people, I'm being vulnerable and sharing the truth with you.

The Lord did lift me up, so I could walk into that situation with my head held high, my spirit strong, and with the love of God in my heart and spirit. By the time it was over, the problem was conquered, because I faced it head-on and didn't let it push me backwards. I'm not bragging about doing this in my power. My own power was as wimpy as a little puppy dog. I kid you not. I was whining inside until the Holy Spirit got hold of me.

Do you remember what Moses said to God, "Lord, if You will go with me I'll go, as long as I know You are with me I can step into this situation." Do you remember the Hebrew boys who were confident if they were thrown into the fiery furnace their God would go with them in there? Daniel knew if he went to the lion's den, God would rescue him from the lions.

Boldness means to move in divine relationship with God in assurance and confidence. Boldness allows us to do what God tells us to do when someone else, or our inner man may be telling us not to do it. We face the enemy or the problem because we know God will empower us and see us through to victory. We need boldness in our world today, and we need it in our hearts as Christians. God has given me a new boldness to speak the truth in love when it needs to be spoken. Every born-again believer should speak boldly each time God gives opportunity.

We are living in a world now where people in sin are not afraid to share details of their lives with us. They may make excuses, "Well, this is just the way I am, you can either like it or lump it." They boldly declare their sins. Why not boldly declare who we are, the sons and daughters of the Living God? "I belong to the King and I have life and freedom in Him. I have the anointing of God, and you can have it too." Be bold enough to share the Word of God in love.

We are living in a season which demands boldness, and God expects believers to walk in boldness and be His bold witnesses. He doesn't say we are to be brash, or tear another person apart because of their sin. God's boldness is coupled with love, and perfect love casts out all fear (I John 4:18). When fear is gone, love brings boldness, and we can walk into any situation and explain what the Word of God really says about this. "I want to help you," and "Thus saith the Lord..." These aren't my words or opinions, but God's words. If you will do this, God will bring a victory for you. Boldness doesn't declare, "You are going to hell!" Boldness states, "Hey, I know Someone who can help you!" Boldness states, "Jesus changed my life, and He can change yours too." Too many Christians are afraid to tell others about the transformation of their lives. That is because the devil challenges us when we try to live up to God's expectation for us, especially telling others about our hope. Boldness declares, "I love you and I love the Lord, and He has an answer for you. Your life can be changed and transformed when you begin walking on a new path with God and leave the old garbage behind. You will have joy in place of hate, peace in place of turmoil in your life."

"When they saw the boldness of Peter and John . . . they realized they had been with Jesus." (Acts 4:13)

The lame man was healed, and Peter and John were being interrogated about it. The people could see the two men's boldness and realized they'd been with Jesus. "Hey, there's something different about these two guys. They are normally wimpy types. They've been with Jesus and now they are bold. What happened?" Boldness releases the power of Jesus!

"They stayed there a long time, speaking boldly in the Lord who was bearing witness to the word of His grace, granting signs and wonders to be done by their hands." (Acts 14:3)

The Holy Spirit brings boldness to us, so we can be bold witnesses. We are not to be belligerent or brash, but bold, assured, and confident when we speak the Name of Jesus to someone, and that is because we can depend upon the Spirit of the Lord to touch them.

I have been the Chaplain for the Billings Outlaws team. I showed up a little early for their first football practice because I wanted to meet and minister to some of the new guys from training camp. Within the space of 15 minutes, three different players came to me with, "Would you pray for me?" Other guys standing nearby probably thought, "This is weird!" You know what I did? I prayed with each of the three right there, in front of the others.

When people ask us to pray about something in their lives, really what they're wanting is for us to pray for them right then and there. It's too easy to say, "Yeah, I'll pray for you," but then go our merry way and forget to pray. I laid hands on those football player's shoulders and prayed, "Lord, in the Name of Jesus, I ask You to intervene in this situation," or "Lord, heal him of the injury he's received," or "God, give him supernatural strength in the Name of Jesus." Our bold witness is proof Jesus Christ is alive and cares about each one of us personally.

"Our gospel didn't come to you in word only, but in power and in the Holy Spirit and in much assurance." (I Thessalonians 1:5)

The Word came in word, in power, and in the Holy Spirit. Boldness and faith are power partners! We boldly declare salvation and forgiveness. We boldly declare the love of God. We boldly declare the baptism of the Holy Spirit. We boldly declare prosperity and increase according to the Word. We boldly declare healing and deliverance.

2. Authority.

The Lord provides us with His own authority for proof the Spirit of God is moving in the world today with authority upon the lives of believers. We've been given this authority power to represent Jesus.

"Love has been perfected among us in this: that we may have boldness in the day of judgment, because as He is, so are we in this world." (I John 4:17)

Look at that! What a powerful Word! We are to be as Christ in this world! The definition of "as" means in like manner, or similar to. As He is so are we in like manner, and to the same degree are we. Did you get that? In like manner and to such degree as He is, so we are to be in this world. The manner of power Jesus operated in is the same manner of power we are to operate in this world. The authority Jesus had, we have! As Jesus operated in authority from the Father, we now operate in His authority.

Jesus proved by His ministry the prophetic Word of God being fulfilled. We are proof of Jesus in this world, and of the Word of God being fulfilled. Say this aloud, "In such manner and to such degree are we!" The Bible says, "***God anointed Jesus with the Holy Ghost and power and He went about doing good and healing all those oppressed by the devil, for God was with Him." (Acts 10:38).*** That is what we are to do!

The Bible doesn't say God gave Jesus only a measure of the Spirit, but that He gave Him the Spirit without measure. He gives the Holy Spirit to us without measure as well. Are you catching this in your spirit?

The Holy Spirit of Jesus gives us divine authority. Jesus walked and lived in divine authority and power, He walked with an anointing over the power of the enemy. Jesus healed the sick, raised the dead, and defeated Satan at the Cross in that divine authority. As He is so are we in this world!

Let me qualify that statement: we are not God. We are not a little Jesus, but we are anointed with the power of the Father, the Son, and the Holy Spirit to carry out the work of Jesus. Jesus didn't come with His own agenda doing His own will. He came to do the Father's agenda, and the Father sent Jesus with the necessary power to accomplish His purposes.

The expectation upon us is to be proof of the power of God to our world in boldness, and with authority. As He was, so are we to proclaim the victories of God, right in this age and in this day. If Jesus is victorious, we are victorious! As He is anointed, we are anointed!

Because Jesus walked in holiness, we too can walk holy! As He is pure, we are also pure, because as He is, so are we. He is love manifested, and we are to love this world. Boldness and authority give dominion over the power of the enemy. We are God's chosen witnesses of Jesus' power to transform our character.

3. Anointing.

"Most assuredly I say to you [Jesus' words], ***he who believes in Me the works that I do shall he do also, and greater works than these will he do because I go to My Father who is in heaven." (John 14:12)***

"You are of God little children and have overcome them because He who is in you is greater than he that is in the world." (I John 4:4)

Witnesses have boldness, authority, and anointing. God never gives His authority without backing it up with His power! We are the anointed of God!

"Works" here means the worker of benefit, or acts. We have so much anointing in God's determined purpose for this day that His expectation is we live in the anointing of God and understand, ***"Greater is He that is in us than He that is in this world," (I John 4:4).*** We can conquer the enemy, utterly defeat that old devil, win people to Jesus, bring our loved ones and family into the kingdom of God, we can lay hands on the sick and they will recover, because we have been anointed with the same power as Jesus! We can do it!

We can stand in the middle of the gymnasium with 29 football players and lay hands on one of them and see God heal him, in the Name of Jesus. We can stand at the water fountain, or the break room at our workplace, lay hands on and pray for someone, and see God move and minister to their life right there. Don't say, "Yeah sure, I'll be praying for you." Don't be afraid of bystanders. Just tell the person, "I'll pray for you right now if that is all right." They may choke for a moment before stammering, "Okay," but usually you will find they do not turn down prayer!

The Bible declares we have the anointing of the Holy Spirit to do greater works than Jesus performed. We are given boldness, authority, and anointing. First John 2, verse 20 confirms it, ***"You have an anointing from the Holy One."***

Tell yourself out loud right now, "I have an anointing from the Holy One." We've been given power, so we can be proof Jesus is alive, and still doing modern-day miracles. It is power to be proof positive the anointing of God is still moving in the earth. Jesus never stopped doing the works of the Father. He's still working, but now His desire is to use us. The Bible guarantees He will draw people to Himself by the power and the anointing of the Spirit of God.

"The anointing which you have from Him who abides in you..." (I John 2:27)

If we will be bold enough to walk in our God-given authority and anointing to prove His victory, the Bible says in Mark 16:17a, ***"signs will follow us because we believe."*** Signs and wonders follow us, folks, because He who abides in us is still performing miracles in our day and age.

"These signs shall follow them that believe, in My Name they shall cast out demons, they shall speak with new tongues. They will take up serpents and if they drink any deadly thing, it will not harm them.

They shall lay hands on the sick and they shall recover." (Mark 16:17-18)

The Word of God declares no deadly thing will harm us. We don't need to feel terrorized. Every day of our life is predetermined and written in a book in heaven, so if it is our time to die, we are going to be with Jesus eternally anyway.

We are anointed, not because I say we are, but because God says so. Speak this out loud, "His Word says I am anointed, I have boldness, and I have authority in the Holy Spirit. I am proof Jesus is alive today and He's still working in this world!" Just as Jesus is, so are we in this world. Say this with me, "As He is, I am. I am, as He is, in this world. I am in a like manner and in like degree, through the power of the Holy Spirit."

Lift your hands with me right now while I pray for you: Father, in Jesus' mighty Name, touch each person reading this. Lord, Your expectation is for us to be the proof in the world today that You are still alive. Your expectation is that we will bear witness of the Good News. You have made us to be the proof Jesus is alive, the proof of miracle-working power still active today, the evidence of God at work on planet earth. I thank You, Father, in Jesus' Name.

The Lord not only wants to empower our life by giving us rights to the kingdom, He also wants to fill each of us with the power of the Holy Spirit, and give us authority over all the power of the enemy. He desires to give us boldness in His anointing.

How many want to be a greater witness than what we've been before? How many want to share greater proofs every day in our life of the anointing of God moving in this world? How many want greater boldness and authority with the anointing of God? If that is you, raise your hands to the Lord and bless Him, and speak this prayer aloud:

Father, fill me up with the Holy Spirit, the power of God, and with the miraculous so that I am equipped to do what You want me to do, to be whom You want me to be, in Jesus' Name. I step forward into You now with boldness, asking You to stir up that boldness inside of me, stir up authority in me, and grant a greater measure of Your anointing inside of me. In Jesus' mighty Name, I believe and I receive and I thank You, Father, and I give You praise, amen.

Now worship Him in your heavenly language. Thank Him for boldness and authority, Hallelujah! Lift your voice in thanks and praise until you feel His glory fill you. Let His praises come from your spirit as you offer Him the sacrifice of praise. He is holy! He is worthy! He deserves the glory due His Name!

Heavenly Father, I loose Your anointing upon every person. I thank You in Jesus' Name for Your divine touch as we walk now in Your anointing, as bold witnesses with authority. Thank You, Lord, that now we will go out to proclaim You, to tell our neighbors and loved ones boldly, "Jesus loves you. He can change your life. Jesus is who you need." Thank You, Lord!

Chapter Four

The Spirit of Love

"For I know the thoughts that I think toward you, says the Lord, thoughts of peace and not of evil, to give you a future and a hope." (Jeremiah 29:11)

The original King James Version speaks of God wanting to give us "an expected end." This is not talking about our demise, but a victorious life. Then He assures us when we pray, He will listen to us.

"I will be found by you and I will bring you back from captivity and gather you from the nations and from the places where you have been driven." (Jeremiah 29:12-14a)

We will seek Him and find Him when we search for Him. His promise is to bring us back from captivity to our rightful place.

I want to talk with you in this chapter about God's powerful truth regarding His intentions and expectations for us as believers. The New King James Version of this Scripture uses the words ***"to give you a future and a hope" (Jeremiah 29:11b).***

The Message translation says, ***"I know what I'm doing. I have it all planned out, plans to take care of you, not abandon you. I have plans to give you the future you hope for."***

This promises I have a future; it is the destiny which God planned for me. We will reach our destination or destiny God has for us. He purposed it, He planned it, and we are going to experience our destiny in God.

I will exegete a couple words for you here. This verse tells us the Lord knows the thoughts He thinks toward us. The Hebrew word for "thoughts" translates as intentions, purpose, or plan. Then the verse tells us we have an "expected" end, which means a hope or longing. God's thoughts toward us are peaceful and good. His thoughts do not include evil, adversity, affliction, distress or grief, although many times God gets the blame for these things when they happen. But they do not originate with Him, nor are they His fault. He is not the instigator of those kinds of things when they happen in our life. His plans and thoughts are always for our good, not evil.

When adversity strikes, remember God did not send it. The enemy is the instigator of adversities and ills with the motive of getting us off track from serving God. His aim is to get us to abandon our faith and trust in the Lord, or to derail us from our hope and future in God, or in what we are believing God to do.

The Lord assures us from this Scripture that His thoughts, intentions, purposes, and plans are for our good, not for adversity, affliction, sickness in our body, or any kind of distress. Those things are the devil's activity. Sickness came into the world with sin, from Satan after Adam and Eve sinned. Distress and grief are not from the Lord, for the Bible says He came to give us Life, and that life more abundantly. The Bible is so specific about this. He declares our latter end will be greater than our beginning (Job 42:12).

If everything is going well and we are satisfied right now in our life, or if we are perhaps dissatisfied with where we are presently, either way, the Bible says get ready, get ready, get ready, for our latter end is going to be greater! The older I get walking with God in the Spirit, the more this Scripture means to me. Our expected end is greater than our beginning.

What God has planned for our future is so much more incredible than what we've experienced thus far! He has plans for us which are more exciting, more powerful, and greater than we've known before. Our latter end will be better than our beginning. If we get off to a slow start in God, get ready, because it is about to accelerate into some things we've never experienced before. Our life is about to explode because God promises the end will be better than the beginning, hallelujah!

When I married my wife 40+ years ago, I thought we had a very good beginning. But I'll tell you what, it's going even better now than it was when we began, (that was for you, Darling). We have more to look forward to, for God promises our ending will be even better than our beginning!

In other words, we may start well with the Lord, but He has thoughts and intentions to bring us into greater blessings. His expected end includes the great things of God pouring from the Holy Spirit into, and out from us in miracles, divine provision, and overwhelming supply. Our expected end is that God is going to pour out His Spirit in our life to a greater measure than we've ever known before. Or perhaps we started out well, stumbled a little along the way on a rough path, but it doesn't matter now because we are back up and headed toward the goal, pursuing our destiny with God. If that is true, our latter end will be better than our beginning.

Don't listen to the devil's lies that once we fall back or fail we will not be able to be successful in God again. No, he is a liar and the father of lies. We are promised a greater end than our beginning. Our latter days will be greater than our former days. That is why the Bible admonishes us not to dwell on the former things (Isaiah 43:18). We are not to consider the past things, for God has greater things in store.

God is doing some awesome and incredible things in our Church, in this Body, because this is the season of God's divine favor. We are living in the outpouring time of God's Spirit, and He has intense anticipation for what He is doing and will accomplish in this world. I'm getting this in my own spirit, too, this intensity of anticipation toward God! It seems like nothing else around me matters anymore. Those old things we used to hang onto in our lives, those pleasures or activities, are losing their luster as we focus more and more on God.

We are living in a season where God is pouring His Spirit out in greater measure all over the world, including right here in this Body, and He doesn't want us to miss what He is doing. His intentions are intensifying. His expectation of what He will do for us is getting greater and greater. I picture it like this: God is at times waiting on us to take the next step, "Come on, My Child, you're almost there, just get over the next hurdle, the finish line is just ahead. I have some incredible things waiting for you if you'll just keep going, keep going, keep going." Come on, folks, let's press into God! Agree with me aloud, "God's plans for me right now are greater than what they were when I started!" We are on the right road to victory and overcoming life!

There was a time when I was waiting for a connection at the Portland airport when I noticed three decked-out businessmen nearby. They wore three-piece suits and fancy shoes. They were talking among themselves about what was going on in Iraq. One mentioned he read somewhere that Saddam Hussein claimed to be King Nebuchadnezzer reincarnated. I kept listening because I wanted to see what track their conversation would take. I knew where I wanted it to end, and that would be for me to get an opportunity to share Jesus with these three men. That hunger in me for harvest is happening all over the world. The fields are ripe for harvest!

In Chapter two, we talked about being filled with the Holy Spirit, the power of God to help us live an overcoming life with freedom, and having a powerful prayer life. We talked about God's expectation that we will be witnesses for Christ, in boldness, authority and anointing. In this chapter I want to speak about being filled with love.

The Lord is doing something fresh in the world today, not only in the pouring out of His Spirit with signs, wonders, and miracles, but also pouring out the Spirit of His love, which is an anointing of His love. Love is such a powerful force in God! Love can destroy the works of the enemy. Even if someone walked in right now with great hatred in their heart, if they encountered us responding in love, it would shut down the angry spirit in them. Love overpowers the enemy.

God is releasing love in greater measure, and we need His anointing of love to counterattack all the anger and hate in our world. We've seen it on TV as we watch both sides of the news about those who love America and those who hate America. (The reason America is so hated is because we love and support Israel. God loves the land of Israel and the Jews; they are His people. And we love them too. It's true! We stand up for Israel and bless them as the Bible instructs.)

In the middle of all this world's anger and hate, God is releasing a dynamic outpouring of His love upon believers. He has an expectation for believers to follow His love example. He is expecting and anticipating us to get so filled with His love that we will walk in the Spirit of His love all the time.

This became so real to me as I was going through a situation with an individual I was ministering to, who all of sudden turned against me. My heart was broken over it. All I was doing was loving them into the kingdom of God, and trying to help them stand firm in their walk with God. Their words and actions crushed both my wife and me. Our first reaction was to back away from them and go the other direction. The Spirit of the Lord spoke to me about it. "Wait a minute, Son, what you are planning in your thoughts is opposite from what I'm doing in the world today, and opposite from My expectation of you. This is the season I am releasing a Spirit of Love. I am releasing an anointing of love."

How will people come to Jesus if we don't love them? We are to love them even if they turn against us! We are to love them even if something arises in them to contest that love. God's Word is declaring by His Spirit, "I am releasing the love of God into the Body because I am expecting born-again believers to be filled with genuine, 100% bona fide, unconditional spiritual love only found from Me." We have all seen enough of the phony stuff around, haven't we? We can see it, recognize it, and other people can see whether it's phony and feigned as well. The Bible says God's expectation of us is to be filled with His genuine, overflowing fullness of His revival love. I want you to see a verse from my loud Bible (the Amplified).

". . . that He would grant you according to the riches of His glory to be strengthened with might through His Spirit in the inner man, that Christ may dwell in your hearts through faith, that you, being rooted and grounded in love, may be able to comprehend with all the saints what is the width and the length and the depth and the height, to know the love of Christ which passes knowledge, that you may be filled with all the fullness of God. Now to Him who is able to do exceedingly abundantly above all that we ask or think according to the power that works in us, to Him be glory in the Church by Christ Jesus through all ages, world without end, amen." (Ephesians 3:16-19)

This is so powerful in the Amplified Version. Verse 17: ***"may Christ through your faith actually dwell inside of you . . ."*** The way Jesus comes to dwell in us in the power of the Father, the Son, and the Holy Ghost, is through the avenue of faith, trust, and confidence in God. Faith is not an intellectual assent to God, nor does it have to do with a particular denomination or church. Faith is a confident reality of our relationship with God that stirs up action in our heart. Faith is a firm trust and belief in God that cannot be shaken.

This Word states Paul wants Christ to dwell in our hearts through faith, or to actually dwell, settle down, abide, and make His permanent home in our hearts. Faith is the beginning place for everything: salvation, healing, baptism of the Holy Spirit, of being filled with love, of trusting God for our finances, and with our finances. Faith is that beginning place; faith must grow and mature in our life as we move with God.

Paul, under the inspiration of the Holy Spirit then goes on to say in ***Verse 17: ". . . may you be rooted deep in love and founded securely on love . . ."***

God's desire is that we will be founded securely in love. Those who don't know the love of God live in insecurity all their lives. They are always afraid of what people will think of them. In the beginning years of my ministry I used to preach that way. I would get in the pulpit, and if I didn't feel like the message was good enough, I'd leave the service with the devil beating on me saying, "Well, the people didn't like that one. You're just not a good preacher." I had to learn to trust the love of God. When the love of God is in my heart, and I obey and do what He says, I am secure about my walk with Him, and as a preacher. My faith isn't dependent upon mere man. I've learned my personal value and worth is not dependent upon anyone but God. I know God loves me, and I love Him with all my heart, mind, and soul. When we love the Lord, we're founded and grounded, rooted, and stable in that love, and that faith drives out insecurity. We can put insecurity right out of our life. We no longer think about what someone may or may not think.

I had the privilege of being one of the chaplains for the Billings Outlaw team for a time. I found my greatest ministry to them occurred when I went in the locker room before the game started, and asked each player individually, "Is there anything I can pray with you about before this game starts tonight?" Many of them asked prayer for their mother or their family, for the game, or for whatever was going on in their life at that time. When I first started praying with them, the guys would look around to see if any of the others were watching while I prayed for them. But that changed. They began searching for me. I'm not kidding. I remember one time when one of the players called out to me, "Come here, I need prayer. Let's go!" We started praying right in the middle of all the other guys, and without embarrassment.

We can't be afraid of what people think about us. We need to be secure in who we are in Christ. We need to be secure in the love of God. He loves us! We can have boldness in Him. We can minister to others in Him, because He loves us! I will be honest with you. When I started praying with the team members at first, I was a little intimidated because I thought some of these guys were looking down their noses, wondering what we were doing kneeling down and praying. Soon the whole atmosphere changed, all because of love, security, a sense of who God is, and who we are in Him.

If we don't love ourselves, love God, and begin to see ourselves the way He sees us, secure in our identity in Christ, we won't talk to anyone about Jesus. The devil will try to envelop us in fear because he wants to destroy our life and witness.

Look at Verse 18: *"... you may be rooted in deep love and founded securely on love that you may have the power to be strong, to apprehend and grasp with all the saints, God's devoted people, the evidence or experience of that love..."* Verse 19 goes on: *"... that you may really come to know practically through experience for yourselves the love of Christ that surpasses knowledge without experience that you may be filled through all your being unto the fullness of God, that is, may have the richest measure of the divine presence..."*

Wow, that is something so powerful. The richest measure of the divine presence comes out of the presence of the Holy Spirit in us. The rich measure is not just the power of God in us. The rich measure really is the love of God in us. We can have all the power of God we want in us, but if there is no love inside, we are missing the main ingredient. Love is the richest measure of God.

I love the power of God, I love the moving of the Holy Spirit, I love the baptism of the Holy Ghost, I love the anointing of God, and I love His presence when He moves through us. But the richest measure, the greater measure, the measure of fullness of that presence is found in the love of God! When God's love overwhelms and moves through us, flowing into our heart, He changes us, transforms us, and releases that same love out of us freely to others. That is the richest measure of the fullness of God.

The Holy Spirit is part of that fullness, and so is the presence of God. But according to the Word of God here, the richest measure of that fullness is God's love! In other words, God's character, His ability, His presence of love comes in to change us. It is a divine God-kind of love. It is characterized by freedom when His love freely flows from out of our hearts by the Holy Spirit. Say these words aloud, "The fullness of love is the fullness of God!"

When the Lord spoke to me to keep loving while in the midst of the heartbreaking situation I mentioned earlier, I had to go right on loving them until God turned the situation around, not by my own strength, but with the power of the Holy Spirit in His love, which is the richest measure of His fullness. I was able to keep on loving them.

The divine fullness of His love also increases some things in my own life. Whether or not there is response from the other party is never the issue. This is where we get hung up. We think if there is no response from the other party, nothing is happening. Not so! There was something happening in me! There was an anointing being released in me of the richness of God's fullness. The richest measure of who the Father is in me began to rise up on the inside of my spirit-man.

God is releasing this anointing of love in the world today, so people will see it and come to Him. The fullness of love changes lives! When people in our lives get out of order (this works with any person), we are enabled to love them into transformation. If my sons did not respond at times to correction or discipline, they would respond to love. They respond to an arm around them from their father who loves them, who takes the time to talk and minister to them. The fullness of love flowing from us has the ability to change behaviors and attitudes.

Will the Holy Spirit change our attitudes too? Yes, because the Holy Spirit provides the love of God to make the transformation. Unless we understand the love of God, we cannot understand the depth of the Holy Spirit of God. The more we love God, the more He releases His Spirit to us. The fullness of love transforms, heals, and sets us free from whatever the devil is bringing against us in an attempt to conquer or destroy us, or to inflict pain on our inner soul-man. The release of God's anointing and love heals us, and then we are able to continue to walk in the fullness of God's love. The fullness of His love restores, enfolds, and empowers us.

THE REALITY OF LOVE

If we grab hold of this revelation, it will powerfully impact us regarding the reality of love. The King James uses the word, "dissimulation," while the New King James uses "hypocrisy" in verse nine.

"Let love be without dissimulation. Abhor what is evil. Cling to what is good. Be kindly affectionate to one another with brotherly love, in honor giving preference to one another." (Romans 12:9-10)

The original Greek terminology also uses dissimulation. "Dissimulate means undisguised or non-hypocritical. The very root of it means the absolute, real thing. I could always tell when my sons would come to me with real love, and I could also tell when they came to me because they just wanted something from me! God commands us to let love be real. He releases real love to us. Dissimulate comes from two words: dis + simulate. "Dis" is a catch word between teenagers and young adults. They say, "so and so dissed me." Or, "I walked over to their group and they dissed me." But "dis" in the Bible implies separation, a negative dispersing, a breaking up, or a sending away. This word says if our love is going to be real, we must be careful not to dissimulate, or be guilty of love that puts up with this one, but not another. We tend to like people who look like us, dress like us, smell like us, or act like us. But when they don't, we tend to shy away, and not have anything to do with them. That's what dissimulating means. It is not a real love; it is merely disguised as love.

I was talking to a gentleman at a wedding I performed. He said, "You don't remember me, but years ago I was in your church. You called my wife and me out of the congregation and spoke prophetically over our lives. Everything you spoke came to pass." (I like to hear that kind of report!) Then, he looked at me while he continued, "You know I felt so much love that day. I'd never been in your church before, but I felt so much love! Is that love still here?" I looked him in the eyes, "Yeah, as a matter of fact, that love is even stronger than before. God's fullness of love is among us, because this is a body who accepts people as they are, and then loves them into the kingdom of God."

I had another person once tell me, "What I like most about the church is the ethnic diversity. I see White people, Native Americans, Hispanics, and Blacks. I see a cross-cultural acceptance in the congregation, and I love it! That is the reason I am here."

Dissimulation is phony, unreal, counterfeit, merely parading as love. It may seem like real love to some, but puts another aside or sends them away. Phony love disses people. I always wondered what dissimilate meant until I studied this Scripture. You can't "diss" me now that I know what it means! I'll just keep on loving you, and I hope I'll love you so much you'll want to get saved!

The other half of the word, "simulate," means to have an appearance of, but no reality. Dis means to send away, but simulate means there is an appearance of love, but it is not real, it's fake and not true, it's not absolute, and people can see through it. It may look like love on the outside, but it lacks reality on the inside.

This Scripture instructs us to let love be without dissimulation. We are to let our love be absolutely real, actual, and not fictitious or hypocritical. That kind of love does not fluctuate by being loving one moment and not the next. It is love mixed with power, love mixed with grace, love with an anointing, love with mercy. That is the kind of love God is releasing for such a time as this.

When people protest or demonstrate against a person or a cause, the Lord showed me they do so because they lack peace in their own lives. They think by having outward peace in the world, they will have inward peace. But you see, inward peace only comes from the love of God. We can't "diss" demonstrators. We must love them because they need Jesus. The only way to true, deep inner peace is to receive Jesus.

LOVE WITHOUT QUALIFICATIONS

In order for love to be real, it must be love without qualification. The Lord put a definition in my heart: "Divine love is the action of affection or benevolence released from, or as a result of the character of God's love in us." Love from the inside Spirit of God has no qualifications attached.

We do things for them without expecting anything in return. They do not owe us anything. I can say positively, but I think I may be getting a reputation in my neighborhood, because when my neighbors are out working on their new yards, I walk over and help them. I just do it because I love them, not because I am expecting anything in return.

When my son Drew was young, he noticed the family across the street (who just moved into their new home), working outside doing landscaping and making preparations for installing a sprinkler system. Drew asked me, "Hey, Dad, are you going to help them?" I thought, "Ugh! I really don't feel like it today!" Yet I knew my son watched me modeling neighborliness, and I didn't want to disappoint his expectation, so I put on my grubbies, and went across the street.

I introduced myself and asked if I could help. The man looked surprised, "Hey, that would really be great!" I helped him for several hours. He couldn't stop talking to me about things in his life. He needed encouragement in several areas, and I was glad I could be of help to him for that aspect as well.

The Bible says we are to love without qualification, so I went across the street to love them. I didn't expect anything in return. I never want anyone to think I'm doing something for them just so they'll owe me. The Bible tells me I cannot live that way as a Christian. There are many who help others with conditional love, which has a payback in mind. "They owe me one." "I'll do this for you, but I expect you to do something for me in return." That is not love. That is actually bargaining, or bartering, or buying something.

If we try to buy someone's love it will never be real. The other person will never come to Jesus because they will think we want something from them.

LIMITATIONS TO LOVE

1. Criticism Limits Love.

We need to take the limits off our love in at least three areas.:

"Without" in the above verse from Romans 9 means beyond the limits, or in other words, beyond the limits of criticism. Criticizing others causes limitations in our own life, not in the person being criticized! Criticism always hurts us first. Criticism limits what God wants to do in our life.

"Criticism" means a reasoned or adverse judgment, or one given to finding fault. Real love does not participate in criticism. Real love will not allow criticism in our mouth, or allow it to live in our heart. Criticism is a limitation which keeps us from entering into the depths of God's love. If we criticize someone, we are really criticizing ourselves, and that results in cutting the life flow of love from our own life. Why? Because what we sow is what we reap!

Criticism brings adverse judgment. Unloving people make judgments like, "If you ask me, it should have been done this way," or "Well, just look at their life. How could they do a thing like that?" Thinking it in our hearts is one thing, but once we speak it aloud, it becomes criticism, and cuts our love line to the Lord. Are you hearing this? This is very important! God expects us to step up to a higher level of love without limitations. He is releasing an anointing of love amongst believers, because He is desiring we would really love just as He loves. True love is not critical.

2. Cynicism Limits Love.

If we are a critic or a cynic, we will miss out on all the things God has for us. As Christians, we must be careful what we say about other churches, about leadership whether in our church or in our workplace, or about people on TV. We have to be careful, so we do not put limitations on ourselves.

"Cynicism" means sneering distrust of people's motives, or disbelief in goodness. Wow! It also means a person's conduct is based on self-interest. There are many cynics in the world and around us. Cynics are scornful or suspicious of the motives of others.

Here is a down-to-earth example of cynicism. "All that preacher does is talk about money and offerings." The cynic and critic always look for a hidden motive, even though the Bible tells us God's motive for offerings is designed to bless us. Paul talked about offerings. He didn't desire a gift for his account, but so those who gave could be abundantly blessed. True love is not cynical.

3. Skepticism Limits Love.

"Skeptic" is defined as those who doubt or disbelieve without conclusive evidence, or one who rationalizes and doubts everything. Skepticism robs us. "I know what the Bible says but I'm still not sure," is skepticism and doubt in action. The devil loves to hear skepticism, so he can steal from that person. True love is not skeptical.

Criticism, cynicism, and skepticism have their roots in jealousy, envy, and pride. Say this aloud, please, "Criticism, cynicism, and skepticism put limits on my life. When the fullest and richest measure of God's love is moving in us, it kicks cynicism, criticism, and skepticism out of our lives, drives away doubt and unbelief, fear and intimidation. Instead of being a critic, cynic, or a skeptic, we are filled with faith that says, "God, I believe You can do anything! If you've saved me, You can save my neighbor! If you've delivered me, You can deliver my child! I have faith that You are moving in my life, and I know You will move in their life, because I am filled with the fullness of Your anointing of love!"

TRUE LOVE

The opposite of the three things mentioned above, and what we are to be filled with is acceptance, forgiveness, and commitment. These three cause us to possess the blessings of God. God wants us to possess His blessings, not be exempted from them. He tells us to go in and take the land, conquer the enemy, and possess what is ours according to the Word of God.

1. Love with Acceptance.

We receive, believe in, and welcome all people with accepting love. I told a football player recently I believed in him. He looked at me strangely for a minute, then told me no one had ever said such a thing to him before. I was surprised! I wasn't referring to his physical abilities, but that I believed in who he is in Christ, and because God has something great for him. That is an example of loving with acceptance.

Does that mean we accept sin? Not on your life! No way, we do not condone sin, but we do love and accept people. We move from liking someone to loving them. "I love you because of who you are, and because of what God wants to do for you. He has a destiny, a plan, and His thoughts are for your good, not evil. There is an expected end for your life. Your latter end will be better than your beginning, therefore, I believe in you and accept you." Why? Because God will take that one from where they are to where He wants them to be, just as He did with you and me.

2. Love Forgives.

"Forgiveness" simply means to pardon or cancel a debt, to cease from resentment, and to give up every desire to punish. Many people get stalled in their Christian walk by a lack of forgiveness. They want all of God's blessings, but are unwilling to forgive. "But pastor, you just don't understand how deeply I've been hurt." Yes, I do understand. Forgiveness is a choice; we choose to live in forgiveness, so our spiritual walk is not hindered by unforgiveness. Jesus forgave us, and because He did we can take possession of the blessings of God. I want you to take possession of His intended blessings.

When we are pursuing the Lord, and bringing people to the Lord, the devil tries to resist and attack us, or tries to put us down. We must consciously decide to get past that, and enter into the forgiveness of God. We are to keep on reaching out and loving people, regardless of what the devil has them do or say against us. God causes us to possess the blessings He has for us when we treat others with His divine love and forgiveness.

3. Love with Commitment.

"Commit" means to entrust, give in charge, to pledge, or to bind. All of these things come from the Spirit of God. We cannot be committed to anything unless we love. When we love with the richest measure of God's love in us, we will also be committed.

I see this operating in people's lives within the Body of Christ through their acts of service. We all love to enjoy the anointing in the worship service. But when it comes to doing grunt work, such as working in the nursery, teaching a Sunday School class, or sacrificing for the kids and youth in the church by ministering to them, many step back, because they say they have too much to do. I'd rather be over committed -- sold out -- so I can walk in the blessings of God and possess what God wants for me. It's part of possessing.

Say this aloud, "I am possessing the blessings of God through acceptance, forgiveness, and commitment." Emotional love is not like that, it reaches out to people in empathy and sympathy, but then turns around and criticizes them with the mouth. Divine love reaches out in compassion, and then builds up and encourages others with faith words.

"Hatred stirs up strife, but love covers all sin." (Proverbs 10:12)

Here is a revelation I've received. Love not only covers sin and hides it, so the Lord cannot see or remember it anymore, but it also means love protects us from sin. In other words, the love of God is stronger in us than sin, enabling us to overcome temptation, lust, and all the power of the enemy. God is releasing that kind of love upon His children. He is releasing the richest measure of His presence and His power. Speak this aloud with me, "Love is the fullness of God in me, and I am believing God moves in me in the fullness of His anointing of love."

Heavenly Father, You are so awesome! There is an anointing of Your love and acceptance, forgiveness, and commitment with us right now. Father, we want to possess all the blessings of God which You have for us. Father, when we see a homeless person on the street, instead of being critical of them, help us to love them. If we should meet someone with earrings, tattoos, and studs in their tongues, instead of being critical of them, help us to love them. When we see those who are battling and struggling with You, instead of being cynical or skeptical about what You can do, help us to trust You to move in them. Help us to love and encourage them because we are filled with gratitude for the richest measure of Your love operating in our own lives.

This is a transformation moment. The Bible says His love is poured out by the Holy Spirit which is given to us (Titus 3:5-6), and that is the love present in this moment. There is a release operating so we can reach our expected end, and we can possess all God wants for us. We can possess our blessings, because of the love of God.

If you have never received Jesus and His peace into your life, or if you are a prodigal son, give yourself to Him now while in the presence of His love. Jesus already won the battle for you. He is drawing you to come into the richness of the fullness of love and blessing He has for you. If that is you, then please repeat this prayer:

Heavenly Father, thank You for sending Jesus to die on the cross for me. Thank You that He shed His blood to cleanse me from all sin, free me from guilt and shame, and give me life abundantly. I ask You to come into my life right now and fill me with Yourself. In Jesus' Name I receive You. Amen.

You just made the greatest decision of your life! God has great things in store for you as you love and follow Him. What you're feeling right now is the presence of God through the anointing of the Holy Spirit. Just let Him touch your heart, way down deep inside. You will be glad you did!

Now for those who already know the Lord and walk with Him, I want to pray with you also.

Holy Spirit, is there anything inside me not letting love be real? If my love dissimulates, resists one but not another, Father, I need to take care of it today. I repent and ask Your forgiveness. I recognize and receive Your anointing of love flowing through my life today. Thank You, Lord. Amen

Folks, God is growing our church with new people, which means we must operate in this anointing of love in greater measure than we've done before.

We need more than ever to walk in acceptance, forgiveness, and commitment. If the Lord is speaking into your heart, asking you to deepen in love, or perhaps saying to you right now, "There is something I want to remove so I can take you deeper into My love," then now is your time to be rid of those things, and receive it from Him. Lift your hand before Him and pray:

"God, keep me real! Keep my love real! Father, in Jesus' Name, I thank You for what You've done in this message, and for touching me, healing me, and delivering me from criticism, skepticism, and cynicism. Because You have touched me, I am no longer critical, skeptical or cynical. All heaven is rejoicing as I commit myself to genuine love. In Jesus' mighty Name I praise You for the love of God released toward me now. Thank You I am now a part of the place where God dwells, where the fullness of God's love flows from me to love people right where they are right now, instead of expecting them to live up to my expectations. Thank You, mighty God, and I ask You in Jesus' Name to loose the Holy Spirit into lives, and stir up the anointing of love in me, which is the richest measure of the fullness of God. I desire it, I want it, I need it, and I want to operate in it. Forgive me for when I've failed or faltered, or if I have limited myself, or limited You. Right now, I take possession of love in Jesus' Name. I take possession of my blessings, believing my latter end will be greater than my beginning. I thank You, Father, in Your mighty Name. I give You praise as You fill me with Your love. I receive Your love, I possess it, and I will share it with those I meet. In Jesus' Name, amen.

I would like to pray for all of us now as we end this chapter. Father, bless Your people, cause Your face to shine upon them, and give them peace. May love so flow from each one's heart, and cause us to be more patient and understanding, slow to anger and quick to love, slow to speak negative and quick to speak positive encouragement, with the love of God into other people's lives. I give You praise in Your awesome Name. We celebrate You and thank You, Jesus, for Your fullness of love shed upon us today. Amen.

Chapter Five

Filled with Love

"For My thoughts are not your thoughts, nor are your ways My ways, says the Lord. For as the heavens are higher than the earth, so are My ways higher than your ways, and My thoughts higher than your thoughts. (Isaiah 55:8-9)

I don't want to miss what God is doing. I want to be a part of what He is doing in this season. I don't want God to have to keep knocking and knocking on our door because we are not hearing His voice. We need to hear the prophetic word of the Lord, and then move with the Spirit of the Lord.

Heavenly Father, in the mighty Name of Jesus, I thank You for the anointing of the Holy Spirit upon me. I thank You, Father, for the revelation of Your Word. Make the Word of God alive to us, Lord, in Your mighty and awesome Name, amen.

When God uses the word, "thoughts" in this Scripture from Isaiah, it means an intention or determined purpose. The Hebrew translation for "ways" means the course of life, or the mode of action.

I want you to see this, as He is saying His determined purpose and intention are not the same as ours, for He has something greater for us than we can imagine.

God has an expectation for every believer, a determined intention, even an intense expectation. What God wants to do for us is so much greater than what we ask Him to do for us. His thoughts are higher, His intention for us greater.

We may think we are living at a very exciting level in Him right now. Perhaps we've never been this deep with Him in our life before. Perhaps we've never experienced such joy, such blessing, and also never have we had as much warfare as we do now yet we know the blessing brings warfare along with it, because the devil tries to keep us from moving forward in the Lord.

Are you excited about where you are with God, and thrilled with the closeness of your walk with Him? God's plan and mode of action for us is even higher than where we are right now. His intention is greater than what we are experiencing right now. If we have financial blessing right now, God's intention is even greater than what we hold in this moment. His course of action includes bringing to us all the blessings of heaven, so we can walk in the dynamics of God, and influence and affect others.

His thoughts and His ways, this Scripture tells us, are higher than the heavens. "Higher" means to soar, to lift up. His plans for us will lift us higher than where we are right now. His thoughts are upward. His determined plan and purpose for our life includes an overcoming life, living in victory, growing spiritually, and conquering Satan.

My biggest struggle as a pastor is when I've preached and proclaimed the Word of God into lives, it seemed the people received it and knew what to do, but for some reason, some continued to battle and struggle, and never seemed to overcome, or get to the next level of where God wants them to go. I pray long for those people, because He expects we will move into overcoming life. He wants to bring us out of religion and into relationship, and then take that relationship into power. He doesn't want us to merely exist, which is what the world is now calling Christianity with no power. God expects, and I want to see, people move with Him into a higher place spiritually.

Since God says His ways are higher than ours, then I must examine my ways, and ask Him what am I doing that is keeping me from going higher with Him. "God, do something in me to step me up in Your power to that next higher place in You. I want to be an overcomer, not just merely make it. I don't want to barely get to the other side, I want to overcome with power, so I can tell the devil from the other side, "You will never bring me back to that place again!"

The Lord's course of life is higher than what I know right now, and I want to keep stepping up. If our lives seem good right now, can you imagine what God has yet in store? God has an intended purpose for us beyond what our finite mind can imagine. In the realm of the Spirit, God desires to take us higher and deeper.

When an internationally known evangelist spoke here,

he prophesied we are only at the edge of what the Lord wants to do with us; there is another step and we will move into something greater, more dynamic than where we've been thus far. We must expect the prophecy to be fulfilled, and keep our faith high.

Each time I come into this sanctuary, I expect the power of God to fall. I expect the anointing of the Lord to be released. I expect signs, wonders, and miracles. I expect the Word of the Lord to change lives. I expect the blessing of God to come upon us, and God expects it as well. He is in anticipation of us, and His expectation of us is high.

We are well able to live up to His expectation, because the Bible states He gives those who know Him the power, the right, and the authority to be the children of God (John 1:12). He gives us divine right and authority, and He expects us to walk in that authority and move into what He desires. Let's get ready for something greater and mightier. Some of us are about to step into it, because I see God about to elevate us and escalate us to a higher level in our corporate life, individual life, our business, and our family lives. Listen, I'm prophesying to someone here. God is stepping us up. I'm going with Him because His ways are higher than mine, His thoughts are beyond mine, and I'd rather live by His ways, rather than my own. We need to step up with Him into a new dimension of His love. He expects His believers to be filled with His love.

A few years ago we were graced with an

internationally known evangelist who held several meetings in our church. Afterwards I asked him a question while taking him back to the hotel. "What is God doing around the world?" He said he saw two things. God is financially reviving those who have a heart to sow into the kingdom of God. He said he was seeing a revival of giving happening all over the world, a revival of God's blessing and prosperity on people who sow seed faithfully, not just once in a while when they have a need. He wasn't talking about "panic blessing." Too many times we wait until a problem occurs, panic, and then we start sowing, hoping for a harvest really quickly. Listen, we can't get a quick harvest that way. We get quick harvests by faithfully, faithfully, faithfully sowing, sowing, sowing. Then God brings in the harvest. Jesse said he sees a revival of that anointing of God producing 30-, 60- and 100-fold harvests.

Then he spoke of the second thing, which really stirred me up, because it is what God is speaking to my own spirit. God is also releasing the Spirit of His love and power across the world, not only in the hearts of believers, but also upon the lost, those bound by fear, and those who are panicking about what is going on in our world today.

People are fearful and frightened. He also spoke of the increased release of the love of God filling the earth. I leapt in my spirit when he said this, because we've been seeing and talking about this too. The Spirit of the Lord is releasing the anointed character of God into His people, and into those who are fearful. He is setting people free to walk in the anointing of His love and they are bringing others into the kingdom.

". . . that Christ may dwell in your hearts through faith, that you being rooted and grounded in love may be able to comprehend with all the saints what is the width, length, depth and height, and to know the love of Christ which passes knowledge, that you may be filled with all the fullness of God." (Ephesians 3:17-19)

"Fullness" has to do with the Holy Spirit, but also with the love of God, or His character of love. The fullness of love is the fullness of God to transform, heal, restore, and empower us. We talked in the last chapter about the reality of love, loving without qualification, and love that sacrifices self. In this chapter, I want to talk to you about whom to love, and then the results of love. I want you to see this fullness of God's love which He wants to release in the power of His Spirit. There is a revival happening in places of this world as God releases His anointing of love. I want us to see the purpose for it, because there is a reason it is happening. The anointing of love isn't just to make us feel warm and fuzzy, although it certainly does.

WHO TO LOVE

The crowd was testing Jesus when a lawyer posed a question of Him:

"Teacher, which is the greatest commandment in the law? Jesus said to him, 'You shall love the Lord your God with all your heart, with all your soul, and with

all your mind. This is the first and great commandment, and the second is like it. You shall love your neighbor as yourself.' On these two commandments hang all the law and the prophets." (Matthew 22:36-40)

Jesus explains everything in our life hinges on these two commandments, loving God and loving our neighbor as we love ourselves. The Greek text shows the "law" He's talking about are principles, or regulations. By that I mean all the spiritual principles contained in God's Word. All the spiritual principles of blessing, of prosperity, of protection, of God moving in and through our lives, His provision, all of the law or principles of God hang or balance on, or work, are based on these two commandments.

What Jesus is saying is if we want Him to move in our life in a greater spiritual way, we must first walk in the commandment to love God wholeheartedly, and to love our neighbors. God holds back meeting our financial need if we are not treating someone else right. If we are treating our neighbor like dirt, but expect God to prosper us, it won't happen. Jesus told the crowd and us, all the other principles of the Bible hang on these two commandments.

We are not fully in love with God if we use Him as a sort of escape mechanism, calling upon Him only when we have a need. We will not experience His victory until we first love God. All the principles of God's deliverance and victory for our lives hang on these two commandments to love God, and love our neighbor. There are powerful blessings inherent in these two issues. We are, first of all, to love God with everything within us. Chapter 13 of Corinthians says we are to love without expecting anything in return, but if we are without love the Bible says we are nothing. We may think we are something, and we may think we are doing something good, but if we're not loving, we are really nothing. We may have the greatest abilities in the world, but if we do not have love, we won't have our needs met. All the principles or spiritual laws of blessing hang on our actions of love.

"Love is the fulfillment of the Law," according to Romans 13:10b. If all the law hangs upon these commandments and love is the fulfillment of that law, then we must open our lives, so the blessing of God can flow in as we love Him and love our neighbor. Love is the fulfillment of the law. Each time we love someone, every other principle in the Word becomes alive to us, and God fulfills His Word for us, because we are operating in the principle of the law of love.

We must get this deep into our spirits because our future hangs on these two commandments. Our financial blessing hinges upon these two commitments of loving God and loving our neighbor. If we are only giving to God because we have need but not because of love, we will struggle getting our needs met until our motive is right. "God, I love You and I'll obey Your Word. I'll do what the Word of God says about giving my tithe and offering, because I love You and I know out of that love comes all the other principles of the

Word of God." God is true to His Word and will make sure it happens for us. We will experience what we're believing God to do; namely, love Him and also love our neighbor. Say it aloud, "Love fulfills the Law." The Amplified Bible tells us love meets all the requirements and is the fulfilling of the law. In other words, the Scripture principles produce blessing.

"Love is the royal law of the Scripture," according to James 2:8. In other words, if we fulfill this law we do well, the Bible says, for it is the royal law. "Royal" means in relation to, or regal, belonging to, befitting the Sovereign One. The royal law has to do with what God declared, and requires the character of the Almighty One giving us the divine anointing of His love and His presence.

WHO TO LOVE

1. Love God.

First of all, we are to love God, meaning the Father, the Son, and the Holy Spirit. We love the Triune One, everything about Him, even if He is chastising. We love His Word when He comes to bring us correction or revelation. We love the work of God in our life. We love Him with all that is within us. You are reading this because you love God, and it became an act of love. The Bible tells us these principles will work for us because we love Him. The more we love God, the more His principles work for us. That is the word of the Lord.

When Jesus replied to the lawyer, He used the word, "with" as He spoke about how we are to love. "With" means in company, or in possession of. To love God with our heart means to possess Him in our hearts. To love God with our soul means to possess Him in our will and emotions, so it is He doing the leading. To love Him with our mind means focusing our perceptions, our understanding, and our thoughts on possessing Him. We are to love Him so much we possess Him and have the mind of Christ. We are to love Him so much we allow Him to renew our mind. We are to love Him with all our strength, which means we will possess His ability inwardly and outwardly. We can only possess Him, His power, and His nature, in the power of love.

We cannot conquer without this power of love in our life. We will battle more and struggle more when we do not have that love. Love carries such power and anointing with it, and all the principles of the Word operate according to that love. Our full trust, obedience, and involvement, our full priority and attention, our full allegiance belongs to God. We love God with everything in our life. We make Him our priority all the time. Love is the fulfilling of the law and it is the royal law. Love is the very character of God.

2. Love Your Neighbor.

The Scripture qualified this principle further by commanding us to love our neighbor as much as we love ourselves. I don't know anyone who hates himself so much that they don't comb their hair, brush their teeth, or cleanse their bodies. No, they take care of themselves. Jesus is drawing an illustration for us by commanding us to love others as much as we love ourselves.

How many of you ladies love to go shopping for a new outfit? How many men like to buy new boy-toys? Do you know why we enjoy doing those things? Because we love ourselves. We care about ourselves. I combed my hair this morning, because I care how I look and am all about nurturing what's left of what I have on top! I brush my teeth, because I care about them and I don't want to take them out at night and lay them on the nightstand by my bed! I picked out my clothes this morning, because I care what I look like. I go to the refrigerator, the cabinets, and the table over and over and over, because I care about myself.

We are to love our neighbors just as we love ourselves. "Neighbor" simply means our fellow man, the one sitting nearby, the one across the street, the one we work with, even our employer. My neighbor is the mayor of Billings. He doesn't live right next to me, but he is my neighbor. My neighbor is a homeless person on the street. They are as much our neighbor as anyone. God wants us to understand we need to have loving compassion for people.

Great men of God are great because they have great compassion and love for people. All the blessings of God hinge on love. There is an anointing of love being released in the world today to set captive people free.

God will use us, the Body of Christ, to do His work, if we will do so with compassion and love. We are to give people genuine care and bless them by loving them, just as we love ourselves.

"Walk in love as Christ has loved us and given Himself for us an offering, a sacrifice for us as a sweet-smelling aroma." (Ephesians 5:2)

We are to walk in love just like Jesus. He gave Himself as a sacrifice of love. I've committed myself to things -- sometimes I over-commit myself -- but when I commit to something, I make sure to do what I say I will do. Even if it is a sacrifice for me, I know I must do it out of a heart of love and compassion. It is the same thing Jesus did for me in sacrificing and suffering. I can give some of my time, even though it may be a sacrifice and not convenient at the time, in order to help another. The end result of my sacrifice of love not only touches their life, which is my main motivation, but God is touched and will make sure every principle of His Word operates on my behalf as well, even when I'm least expecting it to happen.

Jesus sacrificed Himself, therefore we sacrifice ourselves to love others. Love is a choice and it is a sacrifice. Jesus sacrificed by giving His life as a sweet-smelling offering. Each time we love, we are serving. Each time we love our neighbor, we are sacrificing. Every time we reach out to another, it is an offering unto God. Are you hearing this? Every time we love or have compassion upon someone, and walk it out in love, it ministers to them and releases the power of

God to us. Serving others is serving God, an offering, a sacrifice, and God will bless us each time we give of ourselves. The Bible says freely we have received, therefore we are to freely give (Matthew 10:8).

The Greek word for "walk" in the Ephesians 5:2 Scripture means to tread all around, or to live, or to be occupied with. Wouldn't it be awesome if for 24 hours per day the only thing on our minds would be to love God and love people? How many know that is not usually the case? If we'll be truthful, usually our lives are all about love me, love me, love me, take care of me. Come on, be human with me! Take care of me, take care of me, is how we occupy most of our time. The Scripture is commanding us to walk, to tread, to be occupied with love, and that means it is a 24/7 idea.

We need to remind ourselves to love 24/7 especially when we are at home, because that is where love is tested. Love is tested behind the doors of our own homes by what happens in relationships within our own families.

We are to be so occupied with love that it causes all the principles of the Word to operate for us. I'll tell you honestly, I want every principle of the Word of God operating for me, not just some of them. God's Word works, if I am working His principles, amen?

By the way, love is not a feeling or an emotion. At times we will slip into emotions and get upset. But love is actually something deep down in our spirit-man, which is part of our character. Love flows from us in every circumstance of life. Whatever pressure is going on, love will come out, if love has the predominance in our lives. If self is the predominant thing, self will explode and demand its own rights: "Well, what about me? What about my rights?"

I remember when one of our sons got emotional one day because his doughnut was missing. I didn't know it was his doughnut. It was just setting there saying, "Eat me, eat me," so I ate it. When my son discovered his doughnut missing, I admitted I ate it. "But Dad, that was my doughnut! You ate my doughnut?" He started showing his emotion, so I apologized to him.

THE RESULTS OF LOVE

1. No Fear!

Love is our "no fear" gear! An attitude of complete trust in God has no room for fear. Fear would like to rule and reign right now with our world in so much turmoil. We all watch the news and see people in panic. My heart yearns to tell them, "If you place your trust in Jesus, you wouldn't feel such panic!" I don't like to see people panic, or get all nervous and upset, because trusting Jesus calms our every fear. When the journalists give us their take about the world scene, I start talking to the television and my family at the same time, "Just accept Jesus and you won't have any fear! He helps you deal with it.

"There is no fear in love because perfect love casts out all fear." (I John 4:18)

There is a revival of the anointing of God's love, because He desires to drive fear from the world. America was still searching for Osama bin Laden in Afghanistan when we began wondering what Saddam Hussein might be planning. While we were still in Iraq, we began to fear Korea's nuclear weapon capabilities. We also had fear about Syria and whether or not America should be involved there. There was fear in people when the news was reporting fear of SARS, a respiratory disease. There is fear the world over, yet the Bible tells us God's perfect love, His more than adequate love, His love possessed with power, has ability to cast out, and drive away all fear. We do not have to be afraid, or live in fear.

Christians are to live in this day and age according to Mark 16:15 more than we ever have before: we are to ***"lay hands on the sick and they'll recover, speak with new tongues, or drink any deadly thing. . ."*** Drink simply means to take into oneself, to ingest by breathing or other forms. When we take our stand on that Word, we are assured there is no need to fear. If we drink in anything deadly, it will not hurt us. If we stand on this promise, we experience an absence of fear. Do we need to take precautions? Sure, we are to act wisely, after all, God created us with brains. But we are not to walk around in fear. Perfect love hurls out all fear. Whose word are we standing on, God's Word, or the word of the world?

"Cast" means to throw violently, or strike down. The love God is speaking of here, love God and love your neighbor, will violently strike down fear. When fear comes against us, the love of God in us will strike it down, in Jesus' Name. God's love throws it out, casts it out, and it will have no part in us because the love of God dwells in us. This powerful, non-emotional anointing of love from the throne of God, drives out all fear.

The only one I know of who can drive out demons is Jesus. It is His mighty power at work, but He uses human vessels, you and me. Jesus has the power to strike down fear. If we are walking in the love of God, possessing and contemplating His love, and allowing it to operate in our life, then that love will strike down all fear. The Bible instructs fear has torment, but love casts it away. Isn't this awesome?

"God has not given us a spirit of fear, but of power, of love and a sound mind." (II Timothy 1:7).

This is the Holy Spirit's doing, giving us a spirit of love in place of fear. Power, love, and a sound mind are in the anointing of love and power, and released in a spirit of love. I was with someone recently who was all tensed up about something going on in their life. All of a sudden I felt compassion for them in my spirit. I reached out to them in love, and just like that their tension left. Why? Because love casts down worry, fear, and anxiety. Thank God, we are experiencing a revival of love!

Can you imagine what would happen if you walked into your place of employment carrying a spirit of love on a Monday morning? Your co-workers are talking about their weekend, then ask what you did on Saturday night. What if you shared with them how fear was cast out from your life on Sunday morning?

"You did not receive the spirit of bondage again to fear, but the spirit of adoption whereby you cry, 'Abba, Father!'" (Romans 8:15)

Many times, we think we have love, but love is not a word thing but an action thing. Love is expressed by our actions.

2. Peace!

God's anointing of love brings peace. It also gives prosperity, quietness, or rest. In the Greek text, it literally means to join to. When we have peace, it means we have been joined to peace. We've been joined to God, and to His love. If one of our sons is aggravated about something, my actions can either anger them, or calm them quickly by love. I can bring peace into their lives with love. When I hear one of them storming around, I enter his room, put my arm around him, talk calmly about his attitude, and love him right out of it. The result for both of us is love and peace.

Isn't that what Jesus did when He stood up in the boat in the middle of the raging storm? The disciples were scared and chided Jesus for being asleep. Jesus stood up in love and said, "Peace, be still!" He didn't stand up and say, "You idiots, haven't you learned anything yet?" He just stood up and said, "Peace." Need I say more about peace? Let me give you of a few more Scriptures:

". . . the fruit of the Spirit is love, joy, peace . . ." (Galatians 5:22)

". . . the God of love and peace will be with you." (II Corinthians 13:11b)

"These things I have spoken to you that in Me you may have peace. In the world you will have tribulation, but be of good cheer, I have overcome the world." (John 16:33)

3. Increased Faith!

The more we love people, the stronger our faith grows. I'm not talking about faith in a facility, in a person, or in a building. I'm speaking about faith in God, and faith in His Word. The more we love God and love people, the more our faith grows and becomes strong. We will know, "Thus saith the Lord," and count on what God says, because of the anointing and revival of love in the world. God's love anointing increases faith. "Faith" is firm trust and belief in God that cannot be shaken.

"Peace to the brethren and love with faith from God the Father and our Lord Jesus Christ." (Ephesians 6:23)

". . . faith works by love . . ." (Galatians 5:6b)

Here is an important truth. If all the principles hang

upon these two commandments to love God and love our neighbor, then it can't help but affect our faith, because faith works by love. Say that with me, "Faith works by love." If we are not loving God or others, how can we expect our faith to be strong when we need to believe God for something?

Faith works by love. "Works" in this context means effective, efficient, effectual, mighty, or active in love. Faith is active. We don't have to stir up faith because it's already in us. It is in the action of love. If there isn't any love flowing, faith is ineffective. We could try to believe anything or everything, but without love, it will not happen until love is stirred. The anointing and character of God desires us to love Him and love people. When we're doing that, we will have increased confidence with every prayer that is answered, because we are loving God and loving people.

4. Anointing!

The result of loving God and loving people is anointing. We cannot effectively minister to people without the anointing of love, nor can we possess an effective anointing without a deep love. The more we love God and love people, the greater the anointing of God, because God knows He can use us to talk to people without condemning them. When we are walking in love, God knows we will not judge, shame, or criticize people behind their back. God knows we will love them, and our love releases His anointing.

"Hope does not disappoint, because the love of God

***has been poured out in our hearts by the Holy Spirit who was given to us."* (Romans 5:5)**

The Holy Spirit releases the love of God to us. You see, love carries an anointing with it. As we worship, the anointing of God moves and responds, because we are loving Him. When our love and worship reach out to Him, He pours out an anointing. Peace fills our hearts. The gifts of the Spirit begin to operate, and people are ministered to and healed. Why? It starts with love, then timidity leaves, fear is driven out -- struck down by the Spirit of God -- because the love of God is poured out by the Holy Ghost.

There are people around us every day who need our love, and especially need the love of God that is in us to break the fear that is in them. They need the love of God in us to bring peace to their troubled situations. Are you hearing this? This is in my spirit so strong! People desperately need us and the anointing of God we carry within! God places us in certain spots for a purpose. We are there for a reason. It is no accident when we walk through tough circumstances. God took us into that situation to bring peace, love, joy and victory there, and to strike down the power of the devil. The perfect love we possess in our hearts casts out all ploys of the devil. The love of God within us tramples the devil back down under our feet where he belongs.

Say with me, "That anointing is in me! I just need to stir it up, in Jesus' Name!" Can you sense the anointing of love coming through these pages right now? His presence is with us as we study about love. His anointing is awesome!

Do you know why people are saved at our altar? It is because of the love of God. It is not because of us. It certainly is not because of our orange carpet! It is because of the love of Jesus. We can overlook many things, including the color of the carpet, when we are filled with the love of God!

There is an anointing of love when we live by faith, love with peace, love without fear, and God is releasing it to us and throughout the earth. He is present to give it to you if you sense you are being drawn into that anointing of love right now. Why not release it wherever you go today?

Chapter Six

Spirit of Holiness

"For My thoughts are not your thoughts, nor are your ways My ways, says the Lord. For as the heavens are higher than the earth, so are My ways higher than your ways and My thoughts [My intended purpose] ***higher than your thoughts. For as the rain comes down and the snow from heaven, and do not return there but water the earth and make it bring forth and bud, that it may give seed to the sower and bread to the eater, so shall My Word be that goes forth out of My mouth; It shall not return to Me void, but it shall accomplish that which I please, and it will prosper in the thing for which I sent it." (Isaiah 55:8-11)***

Read verse 11 aloud: ***"So shall God's Word be that goes out of His mouth, it will not return void; it will accomplish what He pleases, and it will prosper in my life where He has sent it."*** Hallelujah! God has an expectation for each believer. It is intense anticipation. His promise is that His Word to you and me is not going to return void to Him. In other words, it will not be empty; it is not going to be ineffective, but His Word for our lives will be effective. In fact, it produces, He said. His Word produces seed to the sower and bread to the eater. Those words are representative of harvest. God's intention, His expectation for our life in this season is harvest, and harvest in every way. It a harvest of seeing our families come into the kingdom of God, it is seeing our children born-again, it is seeing our loved ones, friends, and co-workers changed by the power of God. It is the season of harvest.

God's Word is going forth all around the world in greater measure than it ever has before in the history of man. It is going by satellite radio, by satellite TV, and by social media around the world into areas that could not hear otherwise. The Bible says in this season God's Word, and all the time we walk in His Word, is not returning to Him void; it is producing seed for sowers.

We must understand that if we are going to walk in harvest, we have to be sowing the seed of the Word into our lives. When we sow into lives, that Word will not return void. Therefore, there will be a harvest. God will make sure our life is not running on empty. He will make sure our life is full. His joy is in the fact that our life is filled with His blessings, in His presence, in His supply, along with our families also joining us in those blessings of the kingdom of God. He wants us to be full.

His Word, just like the rain and snow come from heaven, makes things come forth and bud, giving seed to sowers and bread to eaters (Isaiah 55:10). There is a harvest that God wants us to experience. He wants His Word coming to us from His mouth to produce bountifully.

What God sends also accomplishes what He pleases (Isaiah 55:11). "Accomplish" in the Greek language means to do or to make. In other words, it will become, it will produce a yield for us to receive. It means to bring forth a harvest. God's Word will always bring forth. Say this aloud: "God's Word is bringing forth harvest in my life."

Then this verse said it will "prosper" where God sends His Word. The Hebrew root word for prosper means simply to add to us what we did not have before. Here in the Hebrew it means to push forward, to break out, or to be profitable. In other words, when God sends His Word into our life, it is going to produce, or break forth His divine promise for us.

If we need healing and sow the Word of God for healing into our life, His promise is healing will break forth. If we need financial blessing, sow the Word of God for financial blessing and obey what the Word of God tells us to do, then we will break forth into the victory of the promise of what God has for us. He said His Word will prosper in the thing He sends it to do. It will be effective, it will push forward. When the enemy seemingly shuts a door, God will open a door with the Word. He will push that door right open! He will make a way where there is no way! It is His promise to prosper His Word.

God's intended purpose, God's determined plan, is going to happen. We are living in the season declared in Joel 2:28 of the outpouring of the Holy Spirit, the divine habitation of God coming to minister in and through His people, the divine pouring out of the Holy Spirit. It is so very important that we understand this, and realize God wants us to be so full of His Word and of His Spirit. so that we are walking in His Spirit every day, hearing His voice, following His direction, moving as He moves, walking in the direction He's walking, and moving with Him in the Spirit and anointing of God. When we do, our life will prosper. Say it with me, please, "My life is prosperous when I walk in the Word of God and in the anointing of the Holy Spirit." There is a release of anointing upon us as we do that. God is releasing that anointing in this season of the Holy Spirit's working in greater measure.

I've been serving the Lord almost all my life. I commit my life to Him when I heard His call to the ministry at the age of 12. I grew up as a preacher's kid, and am descended from other ministers. Before that, I was never totally away from Him in rebellion. I had battles, but I never walked away from God. Over the course of my life, I have watched the Spirit of the Lord in the world, in the earth, and what He is doing. I've studied the revivals of the past, I've read about what God is doing right now around the world. Never in the history of the world has there been such a great pouring out of the Holy Spirit as there is now in the earth! Never have I sensed before such a deep awareness of that presence of the Lord, even in my own life! God is always sovereignly doing things, moving and working and performing, because now is the season of the work of the Spirit.

We will be seeing people whom we thought would never accept Jesus not only commit their lives to the Lord, but also get baptized with the Holy Ghost and fire, and become great witnesses and evangelists. They will impact the world and our city, because of this move of the Holy Spirit in this season. God has some expectations for us in this season of the working of the Holy Spirit.

In this chapter, we will talk about God's expectation for us to be holy. There is no need to be afraid of the word, "holy." It is the word *hagios* in the Greek, which has to do with all that God is, all He wants to do in us, His character, His nature, His righteousness, all His power, everything, including His purity and holiness. This is His expectation for us in this season. He desires us to be holy.

The more we live in holiness with the Lord, the greater we will walk in the anointing of that holiness. It is impurities that hold us back. Impurities keep us from experiencing the great move of God. Be holy!

". . . but as He who called you is holy, you also be holy in all your conduct, because as it is written, 'Be holy for I am holy.'" (I Peter 1:15-16)

God does not require something of us that He will not fulfill for us. He is asking us to be holy, even as He is. When He has this expectation of us, He will also give us the power to do what He wants. "Be" means to take on the nature and character of. So, when He says to be holy, He is telling us to take on the character and nature of purity, of sacredness, of blamelessness, of consecration to the Lord.

"Holiness" refers to the actions of a pure life. Holiness is our life walking out what our Holy God is all about. Holiness is the action of our faith. When we step out of the things that are impure into the things of God that are pure, we will then experience the divine release of His glorious presence in greater measures. Holiness is our part. Holy is who God is. Holiness is the action of a holy life. A pure life in the holy God.

Being holy is contrary to the human nature. Our old nature -- our carnal man, our sinful flesh -- does not like the holy things of God. But our spirit calls for and cries out to God for holiness, for holy and pure things for our lives, but our flesh is contrary to that desire. Our flesh would rather be carnal. Our flesh would rather let lust drive it. Our flesh would rather let pride and selfishness control it. Our flesh would rather operate itself. As believers in this season in which we live, God expects us not to live by the flesh, but by His Spirit. With His expectation He also provides the empowerment, which is an anointing to help us walk this life of holiness, or keep us in step with faith, and in a pure life. God Himself is pure, and He releases the anointing to purify our lives.

The truth of the matter is this: we will live, or we will act out of the nature that is dominant in us! If the flesh nature is dominant, then we will live out of it. If the carnal nature is dominant, we will live according to the carnal nature. But if the Holy Spirit nature, God's character, is inside of us and we allow that nature to dominate our lives, we will live by our Holy Spirit-man instead. That is because of God's transformation through the Holy Spirit at work in our lives.

God gives us a new nature -- a regenerated, renewed, or transformed nature -- and it produces the actions of a pure and holy life. There is no way we can make ourselves be pure or holy, we do not have it in us. But when we submit our lives to Jesus and His power to make us pure, His anointing will equip us to walk upright on a straight course. His anointing will help us speak, think, and act correctly according to God's desires. His anointing will help us overcome the lust of the flesh and the temptations of life. Aren't you glad we live in this season of His anointing?

In this season, God is moving in His church upon people to live pure and powerful in their relationship with Him. Here is why:

"We have been born again not of corruptible seed, but of incorruptible, through the Word of God who lives and abides forever." (I Peter 1:23)

When we are born-again through the Blood of Jesus and receive His forgiveness, we then have the incorruptible Word of the living God inside of us! That incorruptible, powerful Word will override a corruptible flesh nature that wants to rule and dominate our life. That incorruptible seed will produce a pure and holy, incorruptible life!

There is nothing corrupt in God's Holy Word. This Word is life, and it has power and anointing. When the anointing of the Word lives inside us, He will drive out that corruptible seed of the flesh nature and cause the incorruptible Word of God to grow up in our life and bring forth fruit of purity, righteousness, and the actions of holiness. "Incorruptible" means non-decaying in essence or continuance. So, you see, God's Word is not void, it doesn't decay, it is not corruptible, it continues to bring forth, it continues to produce in our life. The Word will always produce in our life as we sow the seed of the Word into our heart. The Word brings us to a place of understanding the Spirit of the Lord, in purity and holiness for our life.

Holiness is internal transformation. External holiness is simply acting in a religious way without any inward change. I want you to understand something because there are a lot of people who are professing Christians that only have external holiness - a religion or a religious way of doing things. They want to be looked upon well, but for some reason, no transformation on the inside has occurred. If holiness is only external, it becomes a ritualistic, legalistic lifestyle, and God is not into ritualism and legalism. God is into freedom, into Life abundant, and He wants us to walk in life, not in bondage. He wants our life to be so changed that when people look at us they can see it. We're not like the world, we're not like those who are not serving God, we're not like those who do not know Jesus as their Lord and Master. We are different! There has been a change - a transformation. We don't do the things of the old life anymore. We don't need them or want them in our life anymore, because we've experienced a transforming change inwardly by the incorruptible

Word of the Living God. That Word is inside us, and is now producing life from living seed, causing us to be like Jesus!

HOLINESS IS INTERNAL TRANSFORMATION

Holiness is internal, not external. I could fake it, you could fake it, we all know how to fake it, because we do it all the time. People ask us, "How are you doing?" We always say, "I'm fine. I'm great," faking it even when we're crying or broken on the inside. We are lying through our teeth. We all have that fleshly tendency. But God speaks life through the Word to our internal being. It's not hard to change an external habit when you have an internal transformation! The desire for the old habit disappears when we've been internally changed. We just don't like the old habits anymore, and we recognize we don't need them.

My mother is and was a great example of this principle while I was growing up. My parents limited the things which were allowed into our house, seen with our eyes, anything, any words spoken that were not pure or holy. Even to this day, my Mom has this holy anointing inside of her that recognizes compromise, or could be askew on the television, anything that puts down the Lord, or gives innuendo of sin. Her spirit inside will turn away, "Oh, I can't hear that! I can't watch that!" It comes up from her spirit. Why? Because there is a holiness there that says, "I don't desire to hear or see that. I don't need that to be happy. I don't need that to meet an emotional need in my life."

Come on, somebody! "I don't need to satisfy that craving. I have Jesus! He satisfies every craving of my life! He is the Lover of my soul, and I don't need to look at anything sexual, or filled with innuendoes for entertainment. I've got Jesus who ministers to me!"

God is talking to us, isn't He? It is the season for holy actions. We don't go to the bookstore for questionable reading. We go to the Word of God where it says, "I am your Lord, I am your King. I favor the righteous with My goodness. I encompass the righteous about with My shield. I protect them! I walk in them! I satisfy them with every good thing from My Word!" That is where we get our pleasure. It is the awesome power of the internal Holy Spirit at work in us. Religious activities cannot change the inside!

I could kneel at this altar for hours, and it would never change me. It would only be religious, unless out of my heart I would say, "God, I allow You to work. Holy Spirit, work inside of me." Then the transformation will start and "religiousity" will come to an end. I can sit in my garage, but that doesn't make me a car. No transformation will take place. I can sit in church, lift my hands and shout, and still choose not to put anything in the offering plate. I can do that because I have not been changed inwardly. Change starts on the inside. All the externals line up, however, when there is an internal change.

When God changes us on the inside, we don't want to miss church, or miss sharing the blessing of giving into the offering plate. We wouldn't want to miss the corporate anointing in the church. I wouldn't miss church for anything. I don't want to sit at home, I want to be with fellow believers. David said he was glad when they said to him, ***"Let us go to the house of the Lord." (Psalm 122:1)*** Do you know why? Because he had experienced inside transformation. He encountered God in the house of God over and over. He experienced the transformation of the Lord for his life. The internal transformation says, "I don't want to miss church! I don't want to miss giving my tithe! I don't want to miss the blessing and the anointing of the Lord! I don't want to miss serving God! I will do what I need to do, and do it with joy, because I don't have the desire to rebel anymore! I've got a desire to serve God!"

The reason that religious activity cannot change the inside -- the reason some people still struggle with sin after being saved – is because they are trying to change themselves. They are trying to do it in their own power. They are trying to change the outside without yielding to the Holy Spirit on the inside!

Sin is a heart problem, it is not an action problem. We look at sin because we have done something that causes us to realize we have sinned. It was an act we noticed, but it's still a heart problem, not an action problem. When the heart is right, God will get sin out of our life. When our hearts and our desires are right, the outside will change. The habit will leave, the desire for tobacco leaves, the desire for alcohol or drugs leaves. The desire for the New Wine of the Holy Spirit comes instead! The desires for sex, whether promiscuity or sexual addictions, leaves us, and the desire to love God arrives. It is an inside change. God works it into us, as the Bible tells us, "both to will and to do His good pleasure" (Psalm 122:1 again). When we are born-again, God gives us this new nature. Say it aloud, "I have a new nature! I don't want my old nature! It's dead!"

If we were to take our old nature and set it up alongside our new nature, they could not be compared. It's like shopping at the mall. If we walked into a store and saw an old tattered garment hanging among the brand-new clothes side by side, which one would we choose? Now guys may not care, but ladies do! They would pick the new one. In fact, my wife would probably take the old tattered one to the clerk and tell them someone must have left it on the rack!

Let me ask you this: Why would we want to buy what the devil has to offer when God has so much more? Why would we want to buy into less, when God says there's more? I would not buy a tattered sport coat to wear to make me look humble or holy. No! I'd pick a nice looking new one. You would too! Why don't we buy into the holiness of God, then? Why not buy into His character and His presence, and let Him work in and through us and change and transform us into the goodness of God, instead of carrying around all that old junk that leads us into misery.

Every Fall and every Spring we go through our closets at home. We lay aside those clothes which have shrunk (and believe me, I had an awful lot of them this Spring, way too many! I want to increase, but not that way!) John the Baptist said he must decrease so Jesus could increase (John 3:30). We set aside those clothes we cannot wear because they no longer fit, or perhaps is now out of style, and find a way to bless another with some still perfectly good stuff. That happens to be a spiritual principle as well. We set the old aside to make room for the new.

I confess, I just don't understand garage sales. We make money, but then spend three times as much as we made getting rid of the old at the sale each time we go to the store to buy something new! You've never done that, have you? We need to do that spiritually. We need to say, "All right God, come and help me get rid of this old stuff in me. I don't want to wear this old stuff anymore. I'm tired of wearing this frown from the pressure of this old hidden sin. I'm tired of wearing the guilt and the shame of this heartache. God, I want You to move it back on the devil where it belongs. God, I want to take on Your new."

We know the things in our own life which are sinful. We know what the Spirit of God is saying to us. The Bible says, ***"I set before you life and death. Choose life that you and your descendants may live" (Deuteronomy 30:19).*** Don't choose the old, choose the new! Choose to be clothed in the new nature. Choose to walk with God. The new nature does not continue to carry the old sins because they have been purged, cleansed, washed, blotted out by the Blood of Jesus. They are gone. We've received forgiveness. We've passed from death to life (John 5:24). Old things have passed away and all things became new (II Corinthians 5:17). The new nature comes forth in new life.

I like to walk around my yard in the Spring. I like watching the buds come forth, and I like to watch the leaves develop. I like to watch the buds come to fullness. I have some things in my yard which are not fully transformed yet, but I still like to look at them in process. I like watching the newness, and the new growth and development. It is fresh, new life coming about. It's been dormant and dead in the Winter season, but all of a sudden new life is springing forth. That is what the new nature is like in our life. It is new life springing forth all the time. It is the anointing of the Holy Spirit working in us to change and transform us. One day we can't help but think, "Oh, I didn't know that beautiful thing was inside!" But it is there.

I said to my wife one day, "Honey, you need to go out and look at our flowers. Our bleeding hearts are already this tall, and they are starting to open! They have little heart flowers on them. They are beautiful!" She went out to look at the new life coming up around our yard. We see Winter so long in Montana, so we appreciate new life when it springs up.

There can be Winter seasons in our life also. Some things cause us to go dormant spiritually. All of a sudden God brings new life to what was dead. We need to get excited about it, "Thank You, Lord! New life is coming out of me! I have joy I didn't have before! I've got peace I haven't known for a time! I'm not carrying that pain, sorrow, shame, or guilt anymore.

I've got new life because of the incorruptible, ever-living Word of God!"

It is the responsibility or work of the Holy Spirit to release in us the new nature of the Spirit of God, the Spirit of Holiness. The Spirit of Holiness is produced by the Holy Spirit!

THE HOLY SPIRIT IS HOLINESS

"Not of works of righteousness which we have done, but by and according to His mercy He saved us through the washing of re-generation, and the renewing of the Holy Spirit." (Titus 3:5)

Washing of regeneration and the renewing of the Holy Spirit is the working of God, not our own. "Re" means anew or again, and "generate" means to bring back into being. "Renew" when broken down is re: anew or again, and new: not existing before. The Holy Spirit renovates us by giving us a new nature. We have a nature we didn't have before we received Jesus. Now we have a nature that wants to serve God. We have a nature that wants to love the Lord and please Him. We have a nature that now wants to be pure, to walk as God walks, and to be more and more like Jesus. We have a nature crying out inside, "Make me more like Jesus!" It is the spirit of holiness crying out to be like Him, to walk with Him, and be holy as He is holy.

God's expectation of us in this season is that the Holy Spirit - the Spirit of Holiness - be at work in us. The Holy Spirit is not just for comfort. We look at the Holy

Spirit many times as our escape mechanism. He comforts us when we need Him, or that the Holy Spirit comes alongside us now and then when we get under pressure, or we need Him to do something for us. Every now and then we rely on Him for special guidance. At times we feel His power. We speak in tongues a little bit, and realize His activity. The Holy Spirit's work is much, much more than those things, however. Those things are good and needful, but the Holy Spirit's responsibility is to work the character of God into us.

"Even the Spirit of Truth, whom the world cannot receive because it neither sees Him or knows Him, but you know Him for He dwells with you and will be in you." (John 14:17)

Say these words aloud: "The Holy Spirit dwells with me and is in me." He's with us! He lives in us! The reason He is there is to do a work in our life. Holiness produced in us by the Holy Spirit results when we yield to His work in our heart.

HOLINESS IS GOD'S CHARACTER

"And when He has come, He will convict the world of sin [the Holy Spirit] and of righteousness and of judgment. Of sin because they do not believe in me, of righteousness because I go to My Father and you see me no more, of judgment because the ruler of this world is judged." (John 16:8)

The responsibility of the Holy Spirit is to convict, or to convince us and bring the demonstration of God. He is there to convince us that living for God is better than living for self. He is come to convince us of our sin, and talk to us about the things in our life that will hinder our walk with the Lord. He convinces us of those things, so we will get rid of them. He will remove them out of our life. He convinces us of righteousness, or uprightness of heart. The Holy Spirit convinces us we need to walk in a holy relationship with God. The Holy Spirit will talk to us and say, "This is what I want you to do. This is how I want you to walk." He will bring the Word of God to our memory, speaking it to our spirit to bring us to remembrance. The Holy Spirit also convinces us of judgment, or consequences for sin. The Holy Spirit warns us of consequences. He'll speak to us and say, "Don't do this or that. Don't go there. Don't enter into that thing. You will suffer consequences of death or destruction as a result of that choice." The Holy Spirit will convince us to make the right choice, because then we will know the blessing of God.

Too many times we try to convince the Holy Spirit that what we're doing is not so bad, after all, everyone else is doing it. We tell him this from out of our emotions, rather than out of faith, "I want to do this even though I know it's wrong." The Holy Spirit will remind us of consequences of doing our own thing, and will convince us to act according to God's Spirit in our inner man. He convinces us not to act out of our emotions or from our mind, but to listen to the Spirit of God. The Spirit quickens us toward purity and holiness in our inner man.

"When He the Spirit of Truth is come, He will guide you into all truth, for He will not speak on His own authority, but what He hears He will speak, and He will tell you things to come. He will glorify Me for He will take what is Mine and declare it to you. All things the Father has are Mine, therefore I said He would take of Mine and declare it unto you." (John 16:13)

Let me share something very powerful and bring this all together for us. The Holy Spirit's responsibility is to make us holy. That is why He is the HOLY Spirit. The Bible says He will speak not on His own authority, but will speaks what He hears.

I will use myself as an example of how the Holy Spirit works to make us pure. The Holy Spirit will speak what God tells Him to speak. The Father says, "Holy Spirit, go tell Gail that the thing he said the other day wasn't right, and that he needs to get forgiveness for that and make it right." The Holy Spirit hears what the Father says. He starts working on my heart, turning inside of me. We start wondering why we feel strange about something. Can you relate to this?

Finally, I'll ask Him, "Are you trying to tell me something?" All of a sudden, the Holy Spirit will pierce my heart with a word from God. The Lord talks to me really quickly. He is quick to tell me what is on the heart of the Father, and I immediately know in my spirit He is right. I know it in my "know-er." It is not like God gives me a great big dissertation. He speaks a quick word into my spirit, and I know I need to take care of this matter quickly. This happened just recently. I had to call someone on the phone and ask for forgiveness of that person, because my conversation had not been right. The Holy Spirit convicted me. The person was so gracious on the other end of the line, but I had to obey God, because the Spirit of God convinced me I needed to do this in order to walk pure before the Lord. But if I moved the other way, I would continue sinning in my own flesh.

The Holy Spirit can come even in a business dealing. We feel in our spirit that something is not right. We feel uneasy, but don't know exactly why. When we don't know what to do, we should not do anything! Instead, wait for direction from the Holy Spirit, for He takes from the Father and speaks it to us. It could be a conviction, or a divine direction. I've had God come and tell me, "Do this right now!" When He says it like that, I know I better do it right now. I am not to wait until I get to church, or wait until I get to the office, or wait until I get to prayer meeting.

God may speak to our spirit to pray on the spot. We may give mental assent, "OK, I will," but continue along on our way. When God says pray right now, He means pray right that moment! When He says stop right now, He means stop right then.

I was driving the other day when the Holy Spirit suddenly told me, "Turn here and go in there." I said, "OK," and made a quick turn. I didn't know at the time why the Holy Spirit abruptly told me to turn and then stop, but I did. I walked into the place He directed, and the person looked shocked. "How do you always know when I need you?" I was able to offer him encouragement that day right when he needed it. I hadn't known that, but the Holy Spirit knew. The Holy Spirit will take what the Father says, whether it is conviction or direction, and speak it to us.

Another time, I was driving a guest evangelist back to his hotel. We were talking, and I missed a turn. I thought I could rectify the situation by turning into the alley. My mistake, the alley traffic was signed for the opposite direction. Here I am with a Man of God with me, and I'm going the wrong way down a one-way alley downtown. "I'm sorry, but I was so wrapped up in our conversation I missed the turn. I'm going the wrong way! Oh Lord, forgive me."

I believe the Word of God so strongly because the Holy Spirit - the Spirit of Truth - has convinced me of the truth of God's Word. The Holy Spirit has shown me Jesus. The Holy Spirit speaks what He hears the Father say, because He wants us to walk pure. He wants us living in the blessings. He wants us buying into Him, not buying into the things the world has to offer to satisfy our flesh nature. He wants us liberated. He wants us free. He wants us anointed and empowered. He wants a glorious church.

The more we walk in purity with Jesus, the greater the anointing. We need the Holy Spirit to talk to us. It is not legalism; it is divine direction, divine blessing. The Word of God does not return void, but accomplishes what He sends it to do. The Holy Spirit speaks the Word. He'll give us a Scripture when we are discouraged or confused. He'll speak a word of faith into our heart from the Word of God when we are feeling down or depressed. When we feel alone, He'll come to speak life. He will take what is the Father's and He will declare it to us (John 16:15). He takes the Word of God, gives it to us in a fresh way even though we may have read it many times. He imparts fresh revelations to us.

"Therefore, having these promises [words] beloved, let us cleanse ourselves from all filthiness of flesh and spirit and perfect holiness in the fear of the Lord." (II Corinthians 7:1)

We are to "cleanse" ourselves, which means all that contaminates and defiles our body and spirit, and we are to "perfect" ourselves, which means to consecrate to completeness. Folks, this is not an impossible task. If we become willing, the Holy Spirit will do all the work.

". . . declared to be the Son of God with power according to the Spirit of Holiness by the resurrection from the dead . . ." (Romans 1:4)

We have within us this Jesus, the Son of God with power, alive and at work in us through the Spirit of Holiness, declaring resurrection to us. The Holy Spirit brings life. He gives us the desire to be pure, blameless, and upright. Give Him praise for His Word to us, and for convincing us we can live in actions of purity by the Holy Spirit, and in the power of the Word. Hallelujah!

I want to close this chapter in prayer:
"Holy Spirit, convince me of who Jesus is, and the power of the Word will always be fulfilled in me. Holy Spirit, I ask You to work in me. I allow You to do what the Father has sent You to do. What the Father has spoken, speak into my heart. What the Father has declared, show to me. I open my heart to allow You to work, in Jesus' Name. I will listen to You, and then I will obey You by doing what You say. I'll not do those things You say not to do. I will do quickly the things You tell me to do. I thank You, Father, that the Holy Spirit purifies me, and every day I am washed with the regeneration of the Word and the renewing of the Holy Spirit. Thank You, Father!"

Now give Jesus all honor and praise. Hallelujah!

Chapter Seven

Let's Talk About Joy

"The Lord of hosts has sworn saying, 'Surely as I have thought so shall it come to pass. And as I have purposed, so it shall stand.' That I will break the Assyrian in My land, and on My mountains, tread him underfoot. Then his yoke shall be removed from them and his burden removed from their shoulders. This is the purpose that is purposed against the whole earth, and this is the hand that is stretched out over all the nations. For the Lord of Hosts has purposed, and who will annul it? His hand is stretched out, and who will turn it back?" (Isaiah 14:24-27)

You did not reach this point by coincidence or by accident. Folks, we live in a day and season where there is not much joy. Yet, the Lord has this word for you. "The Lord's hand is stretched out. Who can turn it back?" No one can turn it back. No devil or demon can turn it back. The purpose of the Lord stands forever! Hallelujah! I want us to get that deep within our spirits, because God has a determined end, and it is always for our ultimate good. It is never evil.

I want you to see the Lord speaking in the above Scripture: "Surely as I have thought," - in other words, the Lord's intention or His determined purposes - "so shall it come to pass, and as I have purposed, [which in Hebrew is resolved and determined plan] - and even as I have purposed, so shall it stand and no man can annul it." The meaning of "annul" is to break apart, to tear asunder, to dissolve or divide.

When God speaks a promise to our life, the enemy has no power to dissolve it or destroy it, even though he may try. He may throw a smoke screen at us. He may try to make the situation look hopeless, or that we are going down and not going over. He tries to convince us it is too late, or it is the last minute, or the last hour, but I have good news for you. When it looks like the last hour, or it seems like the last minute, we better start praising God with all our might, because we are about to get our breakthrough. The enemy cannot turn away nor can he change the plan and the purpose of God! Get ready for your breakthrough!

God has an expectation, an intended purpose, and an anticipation for His believers. I want to remind you this is the season of God's release. It is the time of the outpouring of His anointing, and the time of increase. It is not a time of lack or defeat, for we are living in a new season of increase. It is the time and the season of God's blessing. We must get that deep in our spirit, and believe it with every fiber of our being. This is the time of increase, when God is pouring out His Spirit in greater measure and with a greater outpouring of His anointing. He is moving on those who will allow Him to move, and He is moving through those who will not stand in His way but will flow with Him in what He wants to do. There is a release of the dynamic of the anointing of the Holy Spirit in the earth, and He is desiring to release that anointing on us in this time and season. Not only is there an increase in His anointing going forth into our city, into our region, but into the world in this season.

I want to talk about another expectation the Lord has of us. God expects us to be filled with joy. Joy is our new name! Our name is not depressed anymore. Our name is not downtrodden anymore. Our name is not sinner anymore. Our name is not defeated anymore. I don't walk around introducing myself as Gail Defeated, but I've met some people who talk like that. Some don't have to tell me their name, for it is written all over their face. We have a new name, and our new name is joy! My new name is Gail Joy. Woops, I better change my first name! I get letters all the time addressed to Miss Gail Craig. Someone called the church office once, thinking the pastor was a woman after reading my name on the sign outside!

When I speak of being filled with joy, I am talking about joy that is a spiritual force of supernatural transformation and impartation. When God is changing our life, we can't help but have joy in the Spirit. With spiritual transformation, inside there also comes an impartation of the joy of His presence.

The Holy Spirit empowers with joy, because joy is part of the Holy Spirit! If happiness is dependent on circumstances, instead of on the Holy Spirit, then it isn't the joy of the Lord. The joy of the Lord is not dependent on what happens to, or around us. It doesn't matter if our car breaks down, because that cannot steal the joy of the Holy Spirit. It doesn't matter if we hit our golf ball into the pond, tee up again, and it lands again in the pond. The joy of the Lord is still our strength (Nehemiah 8:10). Those kinds of circumstances cannot steal the joy of the Lord residing within us. If we get all upset and angry with issues happening in our life, we need to check where our joy is. If we allow circumstances to get us upset, we have to get our emotions back on Jesus where they belong. Joy is in the Holy Spirit.

We are talking about joy that is inward, exuberant, enthusiastic, excited, and brings strength. These are only found in the Holy Spirit. That joy does not wane or weaken regardless of circumstances, because the Holy Spirit does not wane or weaken. The Holy Spirit is always on the increase in our life. The Holy Spirit is always increasing us in the things of God, so joy is also on the increase, including enthusiasm, inner strength, and a depth in God in the power of His presence.

I want you to understand God is never sad! There isn't any reference in the Bible about our God being a sad God. He doesn't have a sad countenance. He is not depressed. Our God is a glad God. The Bible even says He sings over us with joy (Zephaniah 3:17b)! He is not a sad God. He is a joyful, singing God.

Nor does our God ever pout. The Bible declares He goes out with a shout (Isaiah 42:13). Come on, somebody! When we don't get our way, some of us start pouting. That is our human nature. We pout until we get our own way. Let me tell you, pouting does not work with God. We cannot pout our way to any victory with God. So, we might as well stop pouting, just get hold of the word of the Lord, get the Holy Spirit in our life, let Him fill us with joy, and when something happens, we won't pout, we will go out with a shout. The Bible says the righteous goes out with a shout, with the voice of glory (Proverbs 11:10). We don't walk with heaviness. We live in joy.

God doesn't fear. His Word is clear! I just thought of that. (It's amazing what you say under the anointing!) God is not afraid of anything. He is not afraid of SARS, the respiratory disease, because He is the Healer! God isn't depressed. He's joy expressed! If you're not smiling yet, you may as well start!

INWARD JOY

The inward joy which I'm talking about here comes from a Greek word meaning comfort and well-being. It has to do with inner gladness, pleasure, and delight that never leaves. It never ceases to amaze me that God does something every day for me which gives me great delight. It doesn't have anything to do with food, or even golf. The reason I enjoy when God does this for me is because it increases my joy. Joy has inner strength, gladness, delight, and pleasure. The word Joy comes from two words in the Greek: one is *charis,* which means charismatic, and the other word means character. So, joy is the character of God, and it is His character in the believer. The anointing of the Holy Spirit and joy are joint tenants in our inward being! We don't have to pray and say, "Oh God! Give me joy!" We just need to stir up the joy already in us! We don't have to say, "God, I feel so terrible. Give me joy!" God is just waiting for us to stir the joy He's already given in the Holy Spirit. He would say to us, "You don't have to feel terrible, just stir up the inner delight and pleasure I've already placed inside you!"

Do you know how to stir up joy? Start talking to the Lord, blessing Him, and magnifying His Name. That stirs up inner delight and joy. Joy produces comfort and satisfaction of the heart. We don't get joy by doing certain things.

Catch this! There is a verse in the Psalms which tells us to shout for joy (Psalm 98:4). The shout doesn't produce the joy, but the joy produces the shout! There are inversions at times in the Hebrew and Greek, and it gets twisted in our English. Really, the translation should be, "in your joy, shout!" Joy gives us a shout. I could stand on the Rimrocks which surround Billings and shout until I am hoarse and never get any joy, because shouting doesn't produce joy. It is joy which produces the shout. Joy is already in the anointing of God, dwelling within us in the Holy Spirit.

Joy produces for us. Joy produces a depth of assurance of faith that ignites a cheerful heart. Say aloud, "Joy produces faith that ignites a cheerful heart!" Do you know why we get excited when we see answers to prayer or hear testimonies? It is because the joy within us is ignited, because we released our faith toward the Lord. Faith ignites a cheerful heart and a cheerful countenance. "Things" don't produce joy. I don't get any joy out of wearing ties. None! I might look quite dapper, but I don't get any joy from wearing one. But joy is in me even while wearing a tie.

Joy makes me appreciate what I have. Joy makes me appreciate the anointing of the Holy Spirit, and ignites a cheerful heart. The Holy Spirit is the One who produces joy. That's one of the reasons the Holy Spirit is so valuable to us. He is the One who is joy. The fruit of the Spirit (Galatians 5:22) is love, joy, peace. Since the Holy Spirit produces that fruit of joy, it means joy is in Him. Joy is in the Holy Spirit, so when He is operating in us, joy is also working in us. We don't walk around hanging our chin. We aren't depressed. We can lift our countenance and let the Spirit of God flow out from our life.

Did you know depressed people are looking for joy? That's one of the reasons they go to bars. They're trying to find something that will give them joy, or be around someone who is happy or laughing. They might be under the influence of something temporarily causing them to laugh, but listen, the world is out there looking for those with something deep and solid, something always there.

Those around us aren't looking to those carrying heaviness, but to those walking in the Spirit of God with the joy of the Lord in their heart. God's expectation for His church in this season before He returns is for believers to be filled with the joy of the Lord.

Joy is the Character and Fullness of the Presence of God.

The more we grow in the character of God, the stronger our joy factor becomes, because the condemnation of sin leaves. The guilt of shame leaves. The more we grow in the character of God, the stronger this joy force becomes inside of us. When the enemy is trying to attack, he can't knock us down because we continue standing firm. He can't knock us off our feet, and we just keep on going. He may try to depress us, but we just say, "Hey, I don't need that, devil. I had that, I tried that, it didn't work." If you've tried depression, you know it doesn't work. I don't let that force of depression land, or even come around me. When I feel the enemy trying to get me into a depressed state, I just say, "Get behind me, Satan. The joy of the Lord is my strength, the Spirit of the Lord lives in me, and I'm going to let God rise up strong in me." Joy is the character and fullness of God in our hearts.

"In Your presence is fullness of joy and at Your right hand there are pleasures forevermore." (Psalm 16:11)

David knew what joy was all about. He knew it is only found in relationship with Jesus. We can't have true joy without Jesus. If we try to manufacture joy, it is only temporary happiness. I can make myself happy with something that gives me pleasure in the natural, but it is short-lived. I can watch a Three Stooges comedy and laugh, because it makes me happy for a bit. But fairly soon, that happiness leaves because it is emotional and temporary. It is not spiritual or eternal. Real Joy is a spiritual force and has power in it.

OUTWARD JOY

The Greek word means the outward demonstration of exuberant exaltation as expressed in public worship. Yes, I really found that definition! We don't do stuff to get joy. Joy comes up from out of our spirit. It is more than an emotion. There is an inward joy, and there is an outward expression of joy. Joy is a vehicle for expressing what God is doing in our spirit. Joy expresses outwardly what is going on inwardly!

I love to watch new babies in Christ. When they are saved and God washes away their sin, all of a sudden something comes alive in them that has been dead all their life up to that point. They get excited, exuberant, and they have zeal. Do we still have ours? We need to have the same zeal and exuberance as newborn Christians. I love being aroud those new baby Christians, because they're not afraid to tell others they received a new life of joy from Jesus. They overflow with joy because their sins are forgiven, and their burdens are gone, and they've been set free from drugs, alcohol, and all other addictions. God set them free and they have incredible joy. It gives me great joy to see their exuberant exaltation.

I went to the bank recently after having a great time with the Lord that morning. He had spoken some things into my spirit so powerfully. I didn't realize I was whistling a praise chorus to the Lord when I entered the bank. Perhaps it was on in my car as I drove there, I don't remember. I was still wearing my sunglasses, and I'm whistling, just tending to business. The teller looks at me, and this big smile appears on her face. I didn't even realize I was still whistling, because I was so happy what the Lord was doing with me inwardly. That joy just came out, flowed out, and touched the teller.

Joy is not reserved only for church. Too many of us wait to get to church to experience a release of joy. When we get up to go to work in the morning, let your boss see you are joyful. "I'm so glad I'm here today, Boss! What do you want me to do, I'm ready to go!" Don't laugh. That's the way our staff is. They march into staff meeting, "All right, we're here, Pastor. What are we going to do?" You don't believe me, do you? Well, a guy can speak in faith, can't he?

Joy flows out of the spirit of the inner man. It is an outward expression of divine fullness and gladness that comes as a result of God's presence, His promise, and His power within. I've got a promise from God, and that stirs up my joy. I've got provision from God, and it stirs up my joy, how about you? I've got power from God, and it causes my joy to jump. Hallelujah!

Joy is not dependent on circumstances. Look at this word. "Circum" means sphere, and "stance" means to stand. Joy isn't dependent upon what sphere we find ourselves, or what the devil is trying to encompass or encircle us with. We might say, "Well, I'm just walking through something right now." It's a good thing you said, "through it," because you are going to get out on the other side. Don't you dare stop in the middle! "But, Pastor, you don't understand what's coming against me!" It doesn't matter, folks. Our sphere, our circumstance is where the anointing of the Spirit of God is being poured out. Our sphere of operation is not in the natural sphere.

The economy doesn't dictate our joy. The actions of our President do not dictate our joy. Nothing from the outward sphere can dictate our joy, or lack of it. The Spirit of the Lord alone dictates our joy. Joy does not depend on circumstances, because we are walking in a spiritual force of joy. Situations or incidents which affect our life, or particular cases or conditions affecting us outwardly, cannot affect our joy. Joy is not dependent on any outward thing. Joy is in our heart. In fact, joy dictates our circumstance!

When we walk into a situation where everyone is depressed or under a spirit of heaviness, we can change the whole atmosphere, because of the joy anointing of God in our spirit. Joy is not affected by environment. "You just don't know the environment I have to work in, Pastor," or "You just don't know the people I have to be around." Maybe they're saying the same thing! Do not allow the environment to affect your joy. We make environmental changes in the atmosphere around us by the power of the Holy Spirit. External conditions or surroundings just cannot affect our joy.

Divine joy is born inwardly, looks heavenward, and is expressed outwardly in enthusiasm and strength. Joy divine in us is in the Spirit of the Lord. Our joy always causes us to look heavenward. The enemy wants us to focus in the natural. God wants us to focus on His promises and His Word. The joy of the Lord in us keeps us focused on, "Thus saith the Lord. I will overcome! I will make it through! I will have my breakthrough! I will have my healing! My children will serve the Lord!" Joy keeps us focused on the things in the kingdom of God. "I will prosper! I am the head and not the tail! I am above and not beneath! I am blessed coming in and blessed going out! I am blessed in my kneading bowl and store! I am blessed in my bosom and in the fruit of my body!" We are a blessed people! Why? Because of Joy!

DIVINE JOY

I've found there is only so much joy a body can handle. I'm serious! This is so cool! The Spirit of God is the fuel to our joy, and at times, our bodies just don't know how to handle it. The Spirit of God explodes within us, in character, nature, victory, promise, development, and growth. It is incredible what God can do in a spirit of joy. I just have to walk through the office at times and shout a little bit. I was singing at the top of my lungs the other day while walking down the office hallway. I didn't know the repairman was working on the copy machine. I'm just going after it with the joy of the Lord. This guy looked over at me rather oddly, but I didn't stop. I just kept right on walking and singing. I figured he already heard me anyway, so there was no reason to stop then. I already gave away my secret of joy.

I want you to see something very powerful. The Lord desires to break the spirit of mourning out of lives today. Please turn to Deuteronomy 28, which I think of as the blessing chapter. Of course this is also the chapter where God explains the curses which will overtake us, if we don't follow the Lord's Covenant. We are blessed if we do this, but cursed if we do that. It was the Law which God gave through Moses to the Israelites. The Law laid it all out for them, so they would have understanding. In chapter 28, verse 47, there is something powerful which He speaks:

"Because you did not serve the Lord your God with joy and gladness of heart for the abundance of all things [provisions or supply of God, the more than enough of spiritual, physical, financial blessings] . . ."

That is sobering, and should cause us to stop and thank God right now. God will not give us the greater until we appreciate the lesser. Let's continue:

". . . therefore, you shall serve your enemies . . ." (verse 48b)

Look at the power of joy! Moses and the Israelites did not have, in Old Testament times, the presence of God dwelling inside of them like we do now. They served God by the Law, by a personal decision. God said if they would do this, He would do that, and when they followed His law, they received blessing. We live in the dispensation of New Testament grace in a personal relationship with the Messiah, where Jesus the Living Lord lives inside of us. But because the Israelites did not serve the Lord with joy and gladness, they had to serve the enemy. They operated according to the Law and choice.

This verse says we are to have joy in all things. That means we should thank God for our clothes, our house, for food, our auto, our children and spouse. We are to serve Him with joy for all things, or else we will serve our enemies.

". . . in hunger, in thirst, in nakedness, in need of all things. And he will put a yoke of iron on your neck until he has destroyed you . . ." (verse 48a).

These are powerful words! If we don't serve the Lord with joy and gladness, Satan will come along and cause us lack, cause us to hunger, to thirst, to be naked and destitute, and in need of all things. The devil will put a yoke of bondage around our neck until we are destroyed. Look at this! If we do not stir up the joy and gladness in our life, we are holding the door wide open to Satan. It is like we are purposely inviting the devil to come in and do whatever he wants to do in our life. This is the word of the Lord!

When I saw this in the Scripture, I ran upstairs and told my wife Penna. I had been studying at home, and I went in and started preaching to her. Drew walked in and jokingly asked, "Daddy, are you preaching already? Save it for Sunday!" I kid you not! He's quite the little wit. He's a good son with a call of God upon his life, and I'm not intentionally embarrassing him here. He asks me every now and then, "Dad, are you going to talk about me in your sermon today?" Both of my sons could, however, provide me with plenty of preaching material!

Who brings hunger, thirst, nakedness, famine and peril? The devil! Do you know what lets him bring it? According to this very verse, it is our lack of joy and gladness! We can be born again but not have joy and gladness, which leaves the door wide open for the enemy to bring lack into our life, all because we have forgotten joy and gladness. Without joy, the devil leads us into captivity! Are you hearing this?

God's expectation for us is abundance of all His promised blessings with joy and gladness of heart. I believe we, at times, do not get answers to prayer because we forget to joy in the Lord for what we already enjoy. We get so depressed over what we do not have, and then we try to get an answer from God, instead of shaking off that depressive spirit by getting excited in the Lord. We just wallow around in that depressed, moody state, instead of stirring up joy in the Holy Spirit as the Word instructs. We could move to a higher place by allowing fullness of joy.

When our circumstances seem beyond our control or ability, that is exactly where God is free to operate. He tells us to keep joying in Him, and He will take care of the rest. How much plainer can I get?

I think I invented another word, "Jollitude." I was trying to use a word to describe my inner joy. But the joy I'm talking about here is not just my word. It's God's Word right here in the Scripture! We are to keep re-joying - rejoicing in the Lord, magnifying God with joy and gladness for the abundance of all things - both for all we already have from Him, and for those He is going to bring.

There is a confession to this joy: "God, I praise You. There is joy in me for what You said You would do for me! There is joy in me, because You said You are my Provider! You are Jehovah Jireh! There is joy in me, because You are My righteousness; I am the righteousness of Christ! There is joy in me, because I have the abundance of all things!" I may not possess abundance at this moment, but I possess it in the Spirit, and it will be manifested for me! Go ahead and declare by faith in His promise that abundance is being manifested for you!

CAPTIVITY

Without joy, captivity comes. It is not a word I like, but I want us to understand it. "Captivity" means one held as a prisoner in bondage, or in servitude as a slave. Do we fully realize we can be born again, know and love Jesus, but still be a slave to some things in our life? It takes joy and gladness to drive out such things as unbelief, doubt, fear, anxiety, complacency, lethargy, and depression. Those things are all a part of captivity. "Gladness" means to be merry-hearted or to be glee-filled. Captivity says we are prisoners in need of all things. Captivity causes despair. Yokes of bondage equal no joy, no gladness. There are two dimensions to captivity, and I want to study these two things closer.

1. Legalism.

The word legalism means inordinate vigor for rules as a means of salvation. If we don't cut our hair right, we will go to hell. If we don't wear the right kind of clothing, we are on our way to hell. If women (or men) wear baubles in their ears or around their necks, God doesn't love them. That's a lie of the devil. Captivity takes us into thoughts and habits which God never wanted us to live by. If someone comes to the house of the Lord and they have a ring in their nose, it doesn't mean God doesn't love them.

I got into a conversation with a young lady at a retail counter some time ago. She had studs all the way down her ears, plus a tongue ring and a nose ring. I'm standing there thinking, "I wonder how she blows her nose?" I've never experienced it, so I was just curious. No, I didn't ask her, but I couldn't help wondering how she could taste her food, or how could she chew anything? The Spirit of the Lord spoke to me right at her counter. He said, "These are her interests, so just ask her."

So, I did! "You have some interesting piercing going on. Some of them are really pretty," but I didn't add, there are just so many of them everywhere. I continued, "I always wanted to know something. May I ask you a personal question?"

She said, "Sure!"

"How do you eat with that in your tongue?"

"Oh, it's easy! It's been there so long I don't even know it's there anymore."

"Well, do you floss it, or how do you take care of it? Do you take it out?"

"No, I just leave it in there all the time."

Well, my showing an interest in her opened the door for me to get into a conversation with her about Jesus. Jesus loves her too. He loves everyone! Jesus calls us to be fishermen; He asks us to catch them, but we are to let Him clean them! If He doesn't like something, He will tell them.

2. License.

This word means to have a total disregard for rules, and the irresponsible use of freedom. We are not to use our God-given liberty as an occasion for our flesh, (Galatians 5:13). We are to be careful our liberty does not become a stumbling block to the spiritually weak, (I Corinthians 8:9).

Both legalism and license attack and steal away joy in our life. As believers, we do not operate in legalism or in license. We live in the freedom of the Spirit. Say it: "We live in the freedom of the Holy Spirit according to the Word of God." This Bible is our covenant, not just a collection of rules, it is our covenant. It is a covenant from God to us, sealed with Blood. Freedom is found in a covenant relationship with our Lord.

There are yokes of bondage the devil tries to put on us. There are captivity issues the devil uses in an attempt to capture us. Captivity scatters us. Captivity fragments our life. Captivity limits and restricts us, because it causes us to be bound. The enemy loves to bind people. We just read Deuteronomy 28 about the enemy coming to put his burden upon people, in order to lead them into bondage and captivity. God's expectation for us, however, is perfectly clear in the following Scripture. God desires to break and destroy bondages for us:

"It shall come to pass in that day that his [Satan's] ***burden will be taken away from your shoulder, and his yoke will be taken from off your neck, and the yoke shall be destroyed because of the anointing." (Isaiah 10:27)***

The yoke of bondage is destroyed by the anointing. We have been dwelling on an anointing of joy! There is a God-released anointing of joy in our hearts.

While I was in the pulpit one Sunday morning, the congregation had no idea something happened to me while I was preaching, but I knew it. Right in the middle of preaching the Word of God, I felt an overwhelming, very incredible, anointing of the Spirit of God upon me. Something inside of me just exploded. It is unexplainable. I don't have the adjectives in my vocabulary to adequately describe what happened to me while I was preaching. All of a sudden it was like every burden I carried, every anxiety, every attack, everything the devil was trying to bring against me, or has ever tried to bring against me, all of sudden was driven out with an explosion! It was like, Boom! Gone!

Just as suddenly as that explosion, I also experienced an anointing of joy. I felt it, I sensed it explode in my spirit. I felt it come into my countenance. I felt my face light up as though I might be smiling. It was such a divine release of the anointing of God, and joy hitting my heart! I went out of that service pumped, not because of what I preached, but pumped because of what I received from the Lord that day. I walked for a few days in that anointing, and it was awesome. I had such an assurance, faith in my spirit, and the Word of God kept coming up in me and out my mouth. All because of joy.

A few days went by and I discovered why I needed that explosion. I encountered something later that week when the devil tried to thwart the anointing, and the joy of the Lord in my spirit. I didn't know on Sunday I was going to need the increased joy and anointing within three days. I had a resurrection of joy in my spirit. If only you could catch this! I had a resurrection of faith. I knew it didn't matter what happened, God was going to cause everything to be okay. I knew whatever I faced I would come out on top. I still know that!

But what I didn't realize was that I would be attacked and confronted by the enemy to try to kill what God just exploded in me. I had to take a stand in the Spirit of the Lord. I had, whether I felt like it or not in the physical realm, to let the praises of God come out of my mouth. Anybody ever been there? I just had to let it loose. I had to speak it forth, declare it whether I felt like it or not, right in the midst of the storm. I now know my praise is what determined the outcome of that battle.

"God, why did this happen all of a sudden? You brought such an anointing through that explosion, and it has taken me to another level with You. Then out of the blue, I am attacked by Satan." God spoke so clearly to me: "The reason I imparted and anointed you with the oil of joy was because I knew what you were going to face, and that you couldn't go through it unless I gave it to you."

"Oh, Lord, You are so right! I cannot make it without You! I receive it, and I'm going on in the power of the Spirit!"

It took a couple of weeks, but this attack from Satan finally broke. I was able to walk through the onslaught in that battle because of the joy of the Lord! The Bible tells us the joy of the Lord is our strength! The yoke is destroyed because of the anointing.

ANOINTING OF JOY

Get ready, because the Lord assured me He wants to release that same anointing of joy to His people right now. The Lord wants to break mourning from people's lives.

In the Gospels we read that Jesus was at the Temple in Jerusalem, picked up the book of the prophet Isaiah, and read from Isaiah, chapter 61: ***"The Spirit of the Lord God is upon Me because He has anointed Me . . ."***

What destroys the yoke? The anointing! Let the devil hear it as you say it out loud, "The anointing destroys the yoke." Now let's personalize it and say, "Because the Lord has anointed me, the yoke of the enemy is destroyed."

"The Spirit of the Lord God is upon Me, because the Lord has anointed Me to preach good tidings to the poor. He has sent Me to heal the brokenhearted, to proclaim liberty to the captives, and the opening of the prison to those who are bound. To proclaim the acceptable year of the Lord and the day of vengeance of our God;" (verses 1-3a)

Why are we bound? Why can't we get free? Why is it we try, but we can't get loose from this thing in our own strength or determination? We need the Lord's anointing. The anointing comes to open the prison doors for all who are bound! It may look bound at the moment, but it will become unbound when you seek Him!

Do we want to walk in the freedom and blessing of God? Look at verse 2, "the acceptable year of the Lord." That is the year of Jubilee, the time of favor! Say this: "I am living in the season of favor! It is jubilee time for me!" In the year of Jubilee, the slaves were set free. In Jubilee, debts were canceled. Some in our congregation have given praise testimonies for debt cancellations - three in the last two weeks!

All the bondages of the enemy are broken in the season of Jubilee. We live in that season! Prior to the return of the Lord, every believer will walk in the power and the victory of the Lord in this season of God's favor. Jesus is proclaiming in these verses the time is coming, is near the end for the day of vengeance of our God. Then He speaks of comfort for all who mourn, and consolation for those who mourn in Zion. Look at this. He is talking about both sinners and saints. He said He would comfort those who mourn, including those who don't know Him, as well as those who mourn in Zion (believers).

I want to show you something very powerful. "Mourn," means to lament, to grieve over, be afflicted by, distressed, overwhelmed with. It is grief, and grief is always associated with death. Do we realize as believers we grieve over situations we don't have the power to do anything about? We lament and mourn our lack. We lament and get distressed by anything we perceive we lack. I'm talking to people today, aren't I? God is about to break this off. It is surely a word from the Lord.

We grieve over our problems. We grieve over temptations, and wish the devil would just leave us alone, or wish he would never tempt us again. We can wish all we want, but the only thing that defeats the devil is the anointing; the anointing destroys yokes of bondage. We mourn because our kids are away from God. We mourn and get distressed, pressed, harassed, and sometimes we mourn because we've done everything we know how to do, and our situation still hasn't changed. We lament, grieve, and get distressed, but look what the Word of God says:

[Jesus came to] ***"console all who mourn in Zion, to give them beauty for ashes, the oil of joy for mourning, the garment of praise for the spirit of heaviness, that they may be called the trees of righteousness, the planting of the Lord that He may be glorified" (verse 3).***

THE OIL OF JOY FOR MOURNING

Jesus came to give the oil of joy for mourning. There is an anointing to break a mourning spirit off our lives today. There is an anointing to break any lamenting. Perhaps we are sick and tired of being sick and tired. There is a spirit the enemy has tried to bring across the world in this season because of terrorism. The devil is trying to unleash a spirit of mourning, of lamenting, even upon the children of God. I've got good news for you! God has an anointing to destroy the spirit of mourning and the spirit of heaviness. We don't have to lament anymore, or get stressed out by it anymore. We may choose to mourn, but we don't have to carry mourning, because God has an anointing to break it off. Heaviness must go! The oil of joy is upon these pages to destroy a spirit of heaviness.

If there is anything in our life which we have mourned, or stressed about, know that is the enemy's work trying to bind us. He tries to get us to grieve over temptation, or grieve over a problem, situation, or circumstance. He tries to get us to lament, and get down and depressed with the heavy burden of it. We are not designed to carry heavy burdens. There is an anointing right now to break and destroy every bondage Satan brought upon us, in the Name of Jesus.

Has the devil held you in mourning in any way? It may be something from the past, or something happening right now. We are in the presence of God, and He wants to break off both the spirit of mourning and the spirit of heaviness. God is going to liberate and set us free today. Instead of shame, the Bible says He will bring double honor (same chapter of Isaiah 61). Instead, we are named priests and servants. We will rebuild and raise up.

"A man has joy by the answer of his mouth and a word spoken in due season, how good it is." (Proverbs 15:23)

If the devil's been lying to you, it is due season to speak a word to him now out of the joy of your heart: "Devil, in Jesus' Name, I am filled with joy, and I'm going through this thing. I am not going to lament anymore, I am not going to be stressed out anymore, I am not going to be depressed anymore, in the Name of Jesus!

Go ahead and lift your hands to the Lord and praise your way to victory. Let's go after it right now! The victory is already won, and the anointing of God is loosed in these moments.

Father, in the Name of Jesus, I bind that lamenting spirit. I bind that stressful spirit. I bind them in Jesus' Name, and I loose the power of God to come upon our readers right now. Upon the authority of Your Word, I loose the anointing of joy, and loose beauty for ashes, in the Name of Jesus.

Praise Him, Praise Him, people! Let joy come from your mouth! Joy and gladness are in you by the Holy Spirit. Let them out now in this anointing which breaks all yokes of bondage in the presence of Jehovah. Hearts are mended as the yoke is broken and destroyed. Do not mourn your lack in any area anymore. Allow the abundance of joy to come out of your mouth from your spirit. Now is our victory! Victory! The anointing breaks every yoke, and sets captives free! Rise up! Celebrate your victory!

Chapter Eight

Filled with Joy

God expects us to be filled with joy even though there are many stresses, distresses, and pressures in this world in which we live. These stresses try to kill or destroy the joy of the Lord in our lives. The Bible says in ***Nehemiah 8:10, "The joy of the Lord is my strength."*** We are going to continue in this chapter about the force of joy, or the anointing of joy. We discussed in the previous chapter mourning our problems and difficulties, and allowing them to rule us, instead of us ruling them. We also discovered the power of God releasing us from that spirit of mourning.

We have attacks which try to destroy the release we experienced in the last chapter, but we also know our joy is not dependent upon any circumstance or happening. Our joy is in Jesus through the power of the Holy Spirit, and that joy is a fruit of the Spirit of the Lord's presence in us.

Father, in the Name of Jesus, I thank You for the anointing of the Holy Spirit right now as we turn our attention to You. I ask that the Spirit of the Lord move and minister to us in a powerful and exciting way, in Jesus' Name, amen.

We also need to be reminded where we sit in heavenly places with Christ in a place of victory. ***"These things***

I have spoken to you that My [Jesus'] joy may remain in you and that your [ours] joy may be full." (John 15:11)

"Joy" means inner gladness, delight, or pleasure. I'm talking about a divine, supernatural joy which is heavenly. It is not a joy we can find in the natural. I can get quite happy when I play a good round of golf, or when I go to the refrigerator for my favorite food. I had one of the most delicious steaks I've ever eaten in my life the other night, but it still did not give me supernatural joy like only Jesus can give. We can enjoy many things, but "true" joy - divine, supernatural joy - is beyond what makes us happy in the natural. I'm talking about the joy the Holy Spirit deposits in our heart, that which is planted there by the Spirit of the Lord. Jesus spoke the above Word to us for a reason. He spoke this promise, so His joy would remain in us and our joy would be full. He gives us the promise of His Word that nothing can steal away His impartation of joy.

I've heard people say (and I used to say this as well until the Holy Spirit gave me a revelation about it), "You know, the devil will steal your joy if you let him." But I've got news for you! The devil cannot take what God has put in our spirit. It is a spiritual gift to our spirit where the devil can't reach. The devil can steal from us in the natural, but not in the spirit. He can't touch our joy. When we are in the middle of a troubling event, we may fail to cultivate joy. We may fail to stir up the joy of the Lord. We may fail to allow that supernatural impartation of joy to be released from our life, but it cannot be stolen.

The devil comes in like a flood with pressure or stress, and before we realize what he's done, we may begin to talk more about our problems than we talk about God's promises. The devil wants us to focus so much on our circumstances, an attempt to keep our eyes from God's victory. If we fall for his ploy, we suppress the joy of the Lord in our spirit, because of our focus. Rather than our spirit and the anointing of God rising and overcoming the situation, we also add to our problem by our own negative confession. The enemy loves it because we just opened the door for him to keep beating on us.

When we feel depressed, stressed, or filled with anxiety, we think joy is gone. In reality, our joy hasn't left us. Joy is ever present in the Holy Spirit, and as long as He is indwelling our life, the joy of the Lord is still there. We just need to get on the offensive against Satan, and stir up the indwelling joy of the Holy Spirit. David encouraged himself in the Lord when he was in danger, or when he became discouraged. He encouraged himself by changing his focus to the attributes, character, and blessings of God.

The Bible tells us to stir up the gifts of God within us (II Timothy 1:6). When we pray in our heavenly language, glorifying God in tongues, that stirs up the spirit of joy that's in the Holy Ghost. The devil cannot steal it, but he will try to push it down so deep we think it's not there anymore. He will try to bury our joy by keeping our focus on our problems. When that happens, it's almost like suffering a death and like we're in need of a resurrection.

The Spirit of the Lord always has joy, and we can walk through any situation in our life with the joy of the Lord and with a smile on our face, even if there is heaviness on our shoulders. There might be torment in our mind, or the pressures of trying to get everything done before a deadline, but even with all that going on in our mind, pressures cannot kill or stop the joy of the Lord we possess in the power of the Holy Spirit and the anointing of God.

What we need to do is simply stir up the joy of the Lord. How many know it's good to laugh? Try laughing at Satan when he gets you down. I get my laughs every morning when I look in the mirror. I start my day out right! I get up talking to the Lord, then walk over to the mirror, and laugh a little bit. Find something to giggle about, it will do you good. God empowers us through the spirit of joy. The promise, the strength, the truth, the stability, the faithfulness, the promised fulfillment of the Word is what should cause us to walk in joy with the Lord.

Holy Spirit joy motivates and empowers. If our day doesn't start out quite the way we think it should, and we want to see it change, then just start moving in the Spirit of the Lord in prayer, worship, and supplication, asking God to stir up joy in us. Soon enthusiasm starts bubbling up. He'll start empowering us. We'll start sensing the glory of God moving through us in a powerful way, and it will motivate us to do what we need to do for the kingdom's sake that day. Joy in the Spirit will lift us up over our circumstances.

Jesus spoke these words for two reasons: first, so His joy would remain in us, and secondly, so our joy would always be full (John 15:11). The only way we can rid ourselves of the joy of the Lord is to turn our back on God. Jesus wants our inner gladness and delight to be in great fullness. When He talks about the fullness of joy, He means not lacking, but overflowing. Say this aloud right now from your heart and with your face, "I am overflowing with joy!"

Jesus spoke this powerful truth to us to give us overflowing joy, and so our joy would remain. One of the most powerful things God works in my life is the Word. When He starts speaking to me out of the Word, my heart is ignited with joy, contentment, and great peace. "God, I'm excited about that Word!" "Lord, that Word is stirring me up!" When He brings revelation, His joy and our joy are both stirred, and will remain. We have the foundation for all things right here in the Word of God. We have His character and His nature in the spirit of our inner man, and He will stir up the joy of the Lord from His Word. Joy is motivated by the Word of God.

Jesus desires our joy to stay full. I can easily describe how to keep joy full. Stay full of the Word of God! Then when we come against a problem, instead of talking about it, we will talk about God's promise. "God, Your Word promises my joy is full. I don't have to doubt this, for it is a promise in Your Word. I don't have to wonder if I've still got any joy. I'm not going to walk around in unbelief or disbelief, Lord. I trust Your Word, I believe Your promise, and that keeps my joy full!" I include praise, worship, and thanksgiving to God. Then I go out looking for some way to bless someone else, because we are blessed to be a blessing. Say that with me, "I am blessed to be a blessing!"

When we thus encourage ourselves in the Lord and in the promises of His Word, as David did, our joy will not lack but overflow. "Full" means to make complete, to level up, and to cram inside. Have you ever felt crammed full of joy? I'm sure you've had times of being flooded with joy. Joy was so crammed in there it just had to come out. Joy cannot be compared with how we feel when someone remembers our birthday, or even at Christmastime. Those things make us happy, but joy is so much more than that. I'm talking about the anointing of joy from the Holy Spirit that keeps filling us with the Word of the Lord going in, and the fruit of the Spirit coming out. That is joy! He said he wants our joy to be totally satisfied, to remain, and to be full.

Look at Jesus' example with me. He was a man of joy even though the Bible also states He was a man of sorrows and acquainted with grief. Isaiah 53 records He took on Himself all our sorrow, shame, and our pain. Do you know why? So, we could have His joy in serving Him. He carried for us every sin, shame, guilt, condemnation, every spirit of heaviness, and any other thing the devil ever tries to put upon us. Jesus dealt with it on the Cross of Calvary. Even so, Jesus was also a man of joy.

I believe Jesus was a happy man. We have pictures of Jesus drawn by artists in years past which make Him look so serious. They almost portray Him saying, "Don't get out of line or you're in trouble!" I've had some of those pictures over the years. Someone also gave me a picture of Jesus smiling or laughing. It was only a photocopy of an artist's rendition of Jesus laughing. I liked it so much I also copied it, and hung them around in the office because I liked looking at Jesus smiling at me.

The Bible says Jesus also sings over us with joy (Zephaniah 3:17b). Even when we fail, Jesus still smiles, because He knows He will bring us up from that failure. Come on, folks! He has the power to lift us up from failure and put us on a path of victory. He joys over us with singing, but that doesn't mean we have license to do whatever we want because He'll just get us out of trouble anyway. What it does mean is we should have joy in our heart knowing Jesus is smiling over us today. "God, I'm walking with You today. You are loving me, and I am loving You. I'm walking in the will of the Lord and in Your blessings. Father, I'm bringing You joy today because I am serving You!"

I experience great joy when I tell others about Jesus. I don't think a day goes by without an opportunity to talk to someone about Jesus. I'm not talking about people who stop by the church with whom I can freely talk about Jesus. I mean when I'm out and about town, mingling with people. I do get out of the church once in a while, you know! God gives opportunities to share Jesus with the public, and it brings so much joy.

". . . looking unto Jesus, the Author and the Finisher of our faith who for the joy that was set before Him endured the Cross despising the shame, and has sat down at the right hand of the throne of God." (Hebrews 12:2)

I just had a funny thought. What if Jesus, when He was being beaten with the cat-o-nine tails, would have just looked at them and smiled? This verse tells us He could endure the cross, because He knew the joy set before Him. Think about this for a minute. He carried His cross up the road with his body, mind, and spirit under a great burden of pain and suffering. I know what the Bible describes about His condition. But what would have happened if Jesus had smiled at people when He walked up that road? Or think about when He was whipped, and had a crown of thorns jabbed onto His head, then nailed to the cross in great agony. I believe, even then, He was smiling with joy in His spirit. Do you know whom Jesus would have been smiling at? At the devil! Every stripe He took, the nails in His hands, the thorns of His head, hanging naked before all of creation between heaven and earth, going through all this public humiliation, He was still filled with inward joy in His spirit. Why do I think that? Because He was looking ahead, according to this verse, to destroying the power of the devil for us once and for all. Go ahead, give Him praise.

Jesus knew one day we would come to find Him and receive Him as our personal Savior, and I believe He focused on that joy as He endured the agonies of the crucifixion. His spirit could rejoice even in the middle of His traumatic situation, because He focused ahead on that future day when we would stand with Him in glory! We will see Him as He is. "There is my Jesus! There is the One I served and the One I loved!" He will say to us then, "Well done, My good and faithful servant! Enter into the joy of the Lord!" He endured it all, because He knew the joy awaiting Him.

His joy through all the cruel punishment He endured was not dependent upon His circumstances. He experienced a deep, inner spiritual joy right through all of it. He despised the shame, yes. But He knew He would make it through and sit down on the right hand of God. "I made it, Father, I'm here!"

We should not be surprised by the fact that the joy set before Him includes all the unsaved. Jesus desires the salvation of even those we cannot fathom, who do great evil, and who hate even the mention of His name, like Communists or Muslims or foreign and domestic terrorists. The joy set before Him includes our next-door neighbor giving their life to Him, because of the testimony of our life. The people we work with are going to give their lives to Christ because of our witness. No wonder Jesus had incredible joy.

I want us to understand something. "The joy set before Him," means to present, or to stand forth, and has to do with being fixed, established, and confirmed. There would be no changes in what Jesus still planned He would do, even though He was cruelly beaten and crucified. The enemy thought he finally triumphed over Jesus. But folks, a divine, supernatural plan had been set in motion long before which could not be changed or destroyed. It was the joy of the Spirit of God in Jesus - the joy set before Him - bringing many souls into the kingdom, and releasing the Holy Spirit into our lives.

The same joy set before Jesus has been given to us! It is imparted into our life by the Holy Spirit. There is joy set before us, and we need to focus our eyes on future glory, rather than on temporary troubles. Say it: "Joy is fixed, established, confirmed and set before me!" What we must do is simply enter into joy. It's already there! That joy is in the Holy Spirit living within us. But we must receive it by entering in. Our joy is set, fixed, confirmed, and nothing can change it. The devil can't, tragedy can't, crisis can't stop it. Nothing negative can hinder it. Our joy has already been established in our divine relationship with Jesus, and the power of the Holy Spirit working within. It's there! Perhaps it just needs you to stir it up!

THE KINGDOM OF GOD IS JOY

"For the kingdom of God is not food and drink but righteousness, peace and joy in the Holy Spirit. For he who serves Christ in these things is acceptable to God and approved by men." (Romans 14:17)

We don't need men's approval for anything, but we certainly need to be acceptable to God. We need His approval. He promises joy in the Holy Spirit when we operate in this kingdom principle. The kingdom is joy! "Kingdom" is the domain of God, the authority of God, or the rulership of God. Something very powerful happens when we allow the joy of the Lord to rule our life. Joy keeps us out of depression, and out of the psychiatric ward. This is God's Word promising the joy of the Lord in our heart, which is that deep spiritual power and truth of the domain of authority and rulership of God.

The Lord began to remind me the other day about an experience which happened years ago in my life. I was remembering a very heavy situation when the devil lied to my mind, beat on me, and told me my situation wasn't ever going to work out, never going to change, or get any better. You've probably been there too, but you didn't stay there, praise God! Every time I went to prayer, this thing hung heavy on me. Every time I came to church, I felt the heaviness of it. It was heavy on me when I tried to study the Word. I remember talking to the Lord in prayer about my situation while laying prostrate on the floor. I was crying out to God, and I found myself whining about what happened. "Just get rid of this for me, Lord!"

There is intercession, and there is whining. I was not interceding, and there was no spiritual impact in what I was praying. I was flat out feeling sorry for myself. Am I reading your mail today? Have you felt that way a time or two also?

I was in my home office whining a little bit when the Lord very firmly spoke, "Get up! (My office here at church is too holy to whine in!) I had the impression the Lord bent over when He spoke to me. I lifted my head, and the voice came again, "Get up!"

I got up on my feet wondering what I was supposed to do next. The Spirit of the Lord spoke to me, "I want you to laugh!"

"You mean You want me to laugh over this? I thought holy laughter had to be stirred up by the Holy Spirit."

"I'm asking you to laugh in the natural."

"Okay. About what?" My flesh was expecting the Lord to tell me a joke so I could laugh at something.

"Just laugh! I want you to laugh in the face of the devil."

The Spirit of the Lord brought to my remembrance, "The joy of the Lord is my strength." So, I began to laugh. It wasn't holy laughter. The moment I obeyed and laughed, the heaviness of that situation broke and joy filled my spirit. It wasn't like I had to laugh for hours. It was just this calm, serene knowing in my spirit of, "Okay, it's done! It's finished! It's accomplished." I experienced an overwhelming sense of the burden lifting off me. I knew there had been a turn-around, a break-through, in which God intervened while I laughed at the devil. I was filled with joy, and I just knew the burden was broken and lifted away. From that day forward, that thing has never been able to come back and put me down with that type of depressing attitude ever again.

I share this with you because I know the devil tries to do things like that to you, too. We need to go to God the right way, not whining, but by recognizing and acknowledging His rulership, domain, and authority. What happened through obeying His command to laugh, even in the natural, was His kingdom of joy in the Holy Spirit became a greater reality than I had known, and the burden rolled away. The pressure was released, the stress disappeared, and the burden of oppression was lifted away. A song started coming into my spirit. I let it come out and began singing my thanks and praise to God, because joy has authority. Say that aloud, "Joy has authority! I will allow joy to rule me."

When the enemy tries to put us down, why join in and play his game? He wants us to drag our chin, but why should we? He wants us to hang our head, but why do it? We don't play his game, because joy has authority. The kingdom of God is righteousness, peace, and joy in the Holy Spirit!

When we lift our head, when we lift up our voice (instead of shutting down our voice), when we lift up our hands, and strengthen our feeble knees, the Bible says the joy of the Lord strengthens us. We can face that situation, fight, overcome, and go through the battle to win the victory.

TWO WAYS JOY OPERATES

1. Joy Brings Sovereign Release and Intervention.

Joy will suddenly release us from captivity. I've found it always has a suddenness to it when joy sets us free. It gives a sense of being finished, full, and complete. Suddenly something happens inside. One moment we have heaviness, but the next moment there is a spirit of joy, an anointing of joy, stirred up inside and bubbling over. We know we are free!

"When the Lord turned the captivity of Zion, we were like those who dream." (Psalm 126:1)

This verse is talking about the children of Israel when they were released from Babylonian captivity. Judah was enslaved, and separated from their home-land. They were captives in Babylon for 70 years. There was an unexpected, sudden release by the king. He told all of Judah they were free to return to their homeland. Suddenly, they were set free from their captivity!

At times, the Lord does something so suddenly for us, but we don't even realize we've been set free. We almost have to pinch ourselves in order to be convinced. It seems like a dream, and we hope we won't wake up in a moment to find everything still the same as it was. Have you been there? We can't imagine the victory really happened. The reason we wonder if it is real is because we've operated in unbelief so long we don't at first recognize God at work. We've been programmed by the devil and by society to live in unbelief for so long we can't recognize when God does incredible miracles for us. This is God's sudden intervention and release.

"Then was our mouth filled with laughter and our tongue with singing. Then they said among the nations the Lord has done great things for them . . ." (verse 2)

When God sets us free, it isn't just for us, but for everyone we meet, everyone we touch, all those with whom we rub shoulders. Even people we meet in the supermarket need to see our freedom and joy.

My wife has this knack. God seems to draw people to my wife wherever we go. The other day she was in a local grocery store. When she entered the fruit department, an old guy said, "Here! Have some grapes." This was not a store employee. This gentleman was testing out grapes, and handing them to others. The Lord brings people into my wife's life like this all the time. Elderly people at times approach her and start talking with her like she owns the place. "Can you help me decide on . . ." or "What do you think of this?" Penna just attracts people. I guess that is how she attracted me, too. Seriously, do you know why they are attracted to her? There is something in her spirit, in her countenance, that draws people. When I first saw her, there was just something in her eyes that said, "You are one handsome, debonair dude!" My heart responded with, "I'm yours, Baby!" Go ahead, laugh a little, but that's how it was.

Joy inside us is not just so we feel good, but also to have an effect upon those people the Lord puts in our path. Or, are you one of those who is so down you have difficulty getting out of bed in the morning? The Lord causes our paths to cross divinely. The Spirit of God desires to use us to lift them up.

The other nations could see the great things the Lord did for the Israelites. The reality set in for the Israelites when other nations began commenting on it. Only then did they begin to express their gratitude to God, ***"The Lord has done great things for us, whereof we are glad" (verse 3).***

I know there are some reading this who have been carrying burdens and heaviness for a long, long time, just like those Hebrews. Perhaps you haven't realized you are in captivity until now. I want to tell you this with a certainty: We are free from bondage! We don't have to deal with our past anymore, because it's gone. We don't have to allow the past to color our today, or dictate our future. Say this with me, "I am not going to drag that emotional suitcase through life anymore. I am done letting Satan deceive me. I am not going to carry this excess baggage any longer. I believe the truth of God's Word, and I receive my freedom in Jesus! I am a child of the Heavenly King and He long ago purchased me from captivity. I will walk now in freedom and joy!"

2. Joy Operates in Sowing and Reaping.

"Those who sow with tears will reap with songs of joy. Those who go out weeping, carrying seed to sow, will return with songs of joy, carrying sheaves with them." (Psalm 126:5-6)

This Scripture doesn't mean the Israelites wanted God to put them back into jail, or put the burden back on them. They are asking Him to turn it again, to bring them out once again.

Joy is reaped either by God's sudden intervention, or by our sowing and reaping. There is another powerful Scripture illustrating this: ***"Whatever a man sows, that will he also reap. If a man sows to the flesh, he will of the flesh reap corruption. If he sows to the Spirit, he will of the Spirit reap everlasting life." (Galatians 6:7)***

In other words, whatever I sow, I will reap. It is a divine law of sowing and reaping. This joy requires our obedience to the principle of sowing. We will reap joy, if we are following the kingdom principle of sowing and planting. We will reap the blessings of God, and joy will be produced. If we are sowing into the kingdom of God, the guaranteed result is reaping joy in the victory of God.

Everyone loves to reap, but usually we don't get too excited about sowing. The Bible teaches we must be sowing in order to experience reaping. This principle affects every area of our life, not only in finances, but in all areas of our everyday life. If we want to reap a blessing, we must sow a blessing. If I want to reap love, I must sow love and kindness. Correct? When we sow a blessing into another person's life, we reap joy. God's principle stands forever that we will reap blessings, joy, and victory. God's divine law includes sudden intervention, which gives us great joy, but also the command to sow and reap, with both shown clearly in the Word. When we reap in joy, we are reaping a harvest according to verse six:

"He who continually goes forth weeping [it doesn't say whining], bearing seed for sowing shall doubtless come again with rejoicing bringing his sheaves [his harvest] with him (Psalm 126:5-6)."

There is a harvest for every sowing. The Holy Spirit within us is our source of power and joy. We keep sowing into God, keep trusting the Lord, keep practicing the principles of the Scripture, and we will reap the joy of the Lord in our life. We'll reap removed burdens. We'll reap removal of heaviness, and being replaced with joy. We reap removal of depression, and experience joy. We sow into the kingdom of God, and receive harvest. We will reap joy in our harvests.

Joy stirred up in our heart causes us to go into the white fields to reap the harvest. Every day our spirit should say, "Lord, I am going out into the harvest today, and I will reap it." It may be a harvest of a soul brought into the kingdom, a harvest for a financial need, or a harvest of the joy of blessing another. It just could be the harvest break-through which we've sought God about for so long. The Bible promises when we sow, we will reap a harvest. If we have sowed in the closet of tears, prayer, and intercession, we need to get up now and go out to reap the harvest.

In our personal life, business life, in our home life, and in our shopping, take on the attitude of going out to participate in the harvest. Go with the thought of reaping from it. We are to be obedient sowers and reapers of harvest.

Personalize the following Scripture to your own situation:

"Thus saith the Lord: Again shall be heard in this place, which shall be desolate without man and beast, even in the cities of Judah and the streets of Jerusalem, that are desolate without man or inhabitant, again there shall be heard the voice of joy and the voice of gladness, and the voice of the Bridegroom, and the voice of the Bride, and the voice of those who will say, 'Give thanks to the Lord Almighty for the Lord is good, His love endures forever.'" (Jeremiah 33:10-11a)

Did you pray those words over your own life today? This is important to speak because the devil is determined to prove our life is desolate. He tries to tell us our business is desolate. He tries to convince us we will not succeed, or overcome. Our promise from God's Word is this: Again will be heard in our house the voice of joy, again will be heard in our business the voice of joy, again will be heard the voice of gladness, and the voice of the Bridegroom (Father and Jesus), and the voice of the Bride (Jeremiah 33:11), which is the church, and the voice of those who will say, "The Lord is good, and His mercy endures forever!" (Psalm 100:5). This is the reaping which is the result of sowing.

We can change the whole atmosphere of a situation by what we speak. We can walk in and say, "Oh, yeah, you poor thing, I feel sorry for you." You know what you did? You added fuel to the enemy's attack.

Or, we can walk in and say, "Oh, listen! God is faithful. He will not let you down. The Lord is good, and His mercy endures forever." Now we are sowing for a joy harvest to happen for them. With your words, sow for something powerful to take place, not only in the life of the individual but also our own life, because the Bible promises with joy we are going to draw water out of the wells of salvation! We are going to draw the joy of the Lord into our own spirit by what we are sowing.

Who are the "those" referred to in the above Scripture? They are those who are not afraid to open their mouth to confess, declare, and praise. Those are faith people. Those people are trusting in the Word of God. Those people are believing God. They are those who don't rely on circumstances, but rely on the truth and promises of God. They do not rely on what the economy or the world predicts, but rely upon, "Thus saith the Lord." The Lord is good, and His mercy endures forever. Are you one of "those?" Say aloud, "Yes, I am one of those faith people. I am one who believes God."

"Of those who will bring the sacrifice of praise into the house of the Lord, for I will cause the captives of

the land to return to their homes as at the first, says the Lord." (verse 11b)

Skip down somewhat to ***verse 12: ". . . and there shall be a habitation of shepherds and flocks . . ."***

"Behold the days are coming says the Lord, and are now here, that I will perform that good thing which I have promised to the House of Israel and to the house of Judah. . ." (verse 14).

Yes, there is divine intervention and it is wonderful, but then there is the law of sowing and reaping. God says we are in the season right now of harvest. It is time to go out and bring in the harvest. Go get your joy! Go bring someone to Jesus! Come on, someone! Sow into the kingdom and let God bring about our harvest, because He promised, "I will perform that good thing which I have promised," (verse 14). I prophesy to you right now in the Name of the Lord: "I will give you, My children, liberty, freedom, and victory. They are yours in Jesus' Name!" Hallelujah!

How many of us need some joy stirred up today? We've been sowing, and now it is time to reap! Some of us need sudden intervention. If that is you, lift your hands in His presence, and start talking to the Lord as one who is bringing the sacrifice of praise. You will be led forth with joy and go out with peace. Start praising Him right now with your mouth. Audibly talk to the Lord and praise Him with the voice of joy, not with the voice of stress, anxiety, or problems. Praise Him with the voice of joy.

"Lord, I joy in you. I am not concerned about the natural, but I am concerned about my relationship with You in the supernatural. You are going to bring about what needs to happen in the natural. You will make it happen. I lift up the voice of joy and the voice of gladness, and my voice with all those who will say, 'Praise the Lord of Hosts, for He is good, and His mercy endures forever!'"

Joy operates in the praises of God coming up from our spirits, and out of our mouths. Some of us need a big break-through today. Some need to get their shout back! Some need to get their voice and praise back. Perhaps your mouth is shut because of the captivity of living in the heaviness of your problem. Now it is the time to open your mouth to the Lord:

"Thank You, Jesus! Thank You, Lord, for freedom, for the anointing, for victory, for deliverance, and for a break-through! Thank You, Father, for divine intervention. Thank you for restoring my joy. And I thank You, Father, that I am also going to reap where I have sown. In Jesus' might Name, I thank You, dear Lord."

Lift your voice with a mighty hallelujah! Do it again! Let the intensity of your gratitude come from your spirit. Now let the Holy Spirit stir up the joy of the Lord in you. Stir up the joy of Jesus in you!

Stand in His presence with lifted hands, close your eyes, and reach up to Jesus. I know some of you have that joy already, but others are having difficulty letting

God be God. I speak especially to the latter: Let Him be loosed from your spirit, because you are carrying too much. You weren't designed to carry such a heavy burden. Jesus carried that burden for you, so you could walk with Him in the Spirit of God and the presence of the Lord. Let praise and thanksgiving come up from your spirit right now. Appreciate Him for what you have, and appreciate who He is in you. Speak your praise and thanks to Him for your freedom! Tell Him, "I love You, Lord!" Go into the harvest field with praise. Sow into your own harvest with praise on your lips.

"But Pastor, I hurt!" Praise Him anyway.

"But Pastor, I don't feel like it." Praise Him anyway.

"But Pastor, I've been rejected." Praise Him anyway.

"But Pastor, you just don't know the struggle I'm going through." Praise Him anyway with the voice of joy and the voice of gladness. Praise Him with the voice of the bridegroom and the voice of the bride. Praise Him with the voice of those who say, "He is good, and His mercy endures forever!"

Your shackles are falling off as you praise Him. The chains are coming unloosed! The captives are set free! Our words are being changed from negativity to pure and holy words, giving glory to God! Can you sense a burden lifted today? I feel liberty ruling and reigning over us as we focused on the Lord just now!

Father, in Jesus' Name, bless Your people today. What a great day. We love and thank You for Your presence. Father, we go out with joy, and we'll be led forth with peace. I give You praise and glory for what You have done this day. In the Name of Jesus, Amen.

Now I recommend you find someone you can bless by telling them of the modern-day miracle you experienced. Tell them you are filled with a joy unspeakable and full of glory. Tell them they can have this joy, too!

Chapter Nine Characteristics of a Joy-Filled Life

[David said,] *"I will praise You for You have answered me, and You have become my salvation. The stone which the builders rejected has become the Chief Cornerstone [Jesus]. This was the Lord's doing. It was marvelous in our eyes. This is the day which the Lord has made, we will rejoice and be glad in it. Save now I pray, Oh Lord, and grant us success. Blessed is He who comes in the name of the Lord. We have blessed you from the house of our God." (Psalm 118:21-26)*

In this chapter, I will deal with the characterizing results of a joy-filled life. God wants His Church, (His people), to be filled with joy. He does not want those who love and serve Him to be depressed, to hang their head, or drag their chin, or be kicking themselves in their Christian walk. He wants His people to lift up their head, and let the joy of the Lord flow out from our spirit, so when others see our life they definitely know something is different about us, and they want it too.

There is much depression in our world. There are so many relying on both legal and illegal mood-altering drugs to fix their lives, to lift them from the pit. I'm out and about in our community, and I can recognize depressed persons when I see them. I can sense their heaviness. The Lord wants them to know Him and to experience liberty, joy, and release of gladness which

He brings to the church. It is not a day to hang our head and be sad. It is time to lift our head and rejoice, looking up because our redemption is drawing near, (Luke 21:28).

Father, I thank You today for Your anointing and for the power of Your Word. Lord, in this chapter, I ask You to make the Word of God alive to us and alive in our spirit. Stir us up, Father, to lift our heads, to lift our hearts, and to lift our praises to You, because Your joy dwells inside of us. I thank You, in Your wonderful Name, amen.

Let's transliterate verse 24 (above) a little bit. The Bible says today is the day the Lord has made. "Day" represents the season, the time. It means full life or full age, or something that came to age of fruition, or harvest bearing. This is the day and the season of partaking of the harvest for our life. It is the season of receiving the promises of God which He has spoken into our life. We stood on the Word of God, and are still standing on that Word of the Lord, we have His divine promise, and we are praising and thanking Him for what He is going to procure for us, those answers He said are ours according to the Word of God. If so, then this is the day of our harvest. This is the season of God to bring it forth for us. This is the season of God's outpouring of His Spirit in the earth.

Say that with me: "This is the season of God's pouring forth of the Holy Spirit into hungry hearts. I am a hungry one." We are hungry for God's pouring out. It is a perpetual season of God's blessing. If we look around the world we might conclude it doesn't look like it, but we do not walk by sight, we walk by faith (II Corinthians 5:7). We don't live by sight, we live by faith. We don't believe by sight, we believe by faith. We stand upon what we know is true in the Word, not on what we see. We believe what the Word of the Lord says.

This is the day, the season of our harvest. Lift a hand to the Lord and say, "Thank You, Lord, that this is the day of my harvest. This is the season of return. This is a season of blessing for me, Lord. I am believing and receiving what You say in Your Word is mine." You just made a good faith declaration.

"Made" in this verse means He has accomplished. One translation says to advance, or to appoint, to bring forth, to become, to bestow. In other words, this is the day the Lord created, He has declared it, He spoke into it, and His Word does not return void, (Isaiah 55:11). The word of the Lord creates everything. He spoke the world into existence. So, when He said this is the day He made, this very day is the day the Lord spoke into. If God has spoken into our day, then there will be a harvest in this season. Go ahead and praise Him! There will be a blessing from the Lord, because His Word doesn't return void. When He speaks it, it will come to pass. This is the day the Lord spoke into. God is speaking into our day every day. Because He spoke into our day with the promise of His Word, that day, that season, that harvest happens. Get this in our spirit, Lord.

This isn't just a day on the calendar. This is the day He declared, the day of victory, of breakthrough, the day for our businesses to rise higher, for our children to get saved, the day for our marriage to be united closer. It is the day for our family to step up to a new level. It is the day for God to pour out His anointing upon us. It is a day of coming out of poverty into His blessing. Today! He has spoken into this day for His good pleasure.

We will rejoice in this day. The primary root word for "rejoice" in Hebrew is to spin under the influence of joy! Rejoice, to spin with joy! That is the literal translation! There will be glee and excitement in this day. Since the Lord spoke into it, let joy be released from our spirit because God is doing something exciting, and He is doing this today. Go ahead and spin around with joy!

I left out an important word. We are to spin under the influence of joy! We need to be under the influence of the right thing. We try many things to influence us and to make us happy. But it is the joy of God residing within believers, the joy of sins forgiven, the joy of having a Jesus relationship, these are the influences promoting joy. In other words, we have a joy-filled response. It has to do with God's charisma of character. We are the most charismatic of people, because we have the character of God within us. I didn't say we are cruise-a-matics, I said char-is-matics.

Charisma doesn't have anything to do with personality. There are some very personality-plus type of people who seem to be "up" all the time, (we just don't see them when they are down). I am not talking about personality. We rejoice with the charisma (the anointing of the Spirit of God) of God's character within us. The joy of the Lord in us causes us to rejoice when God speaks into our day. When He says we will have a better day today than we did yesterday, that makes me want to spin and rejoice. It makes the charisma, the anointing, flow from my spirit and all I can say is, "Thank You, Lord!" Say: "I will, I will, I will rejoice!"

Then He says to be glad in this day. The word, "be," means to take on the nature of. Any time in Scripture we encounter the word, "be," it means take on, become, the nature, the likeness, or in this case to be like God. I will rejoice and be glad means to take on the nature. The Spirit and the character of God is in us, this is the day God is speaking into, therefore, I will rejoice out of the character of the joy in my heart, and I will be, or take on the nature of gladness.

"Glad" means to be gleeful or merry-hearted. In the original Greek text, it means to brighten up, to cheer up, and to merry up. Come on, brighten up, cheer up, be merry because we are victorious.

We take on the nature of gladness. The nature of gladness is a merry heart, full of fun and laughter. I'm not talking about the world's version. The world doesn't know what real fun is. The world's fun is temporary pleasure. The joy of the Lord has to do with the character of Jesus bringing gladness, fun, and a merry heart. It is a response of rejoicing under the influence of inner delight and the character of joy. We respond to the influence of joy.

How many times do we respond to the influence of our emotions, instead? I mean we respond when the devil beats on our mind and lies to us. We respond out of emotion, but God wants us to respond according to the joy of the Lord, and what He is doing in our life. When the stress is on, the joy of the Lord is also on. When the pressure is on, the joy of the Lord is still there, in fact, will rise up stronger than that pressure.

CHARACTERISTICS (RESULTS) OF JOY

1. Love.

Well, that sounds very simple, you say. The "love" we are discussing is divine affection and attachment to the Lord. Here is what I found joy does in my heart. When I release joy out of my life, it causes my heart to explode with love toward God. If I suppress the joy, it is like holding back everything God wants to do in my heart. Whenever I see the teenagers jumping up and down in unison while we are singing praises to the Lord, it increases my joy in the Lord. Some may have looked at them with one eye while thinking, "What do they think they are doing in church!"

When we sing, "I want the joy of the Lord in my life," it releases their joy, and they can't help but to express it by the Spirit. It is okay to bounce or dance in celebration of Jesus! If we suppress joy, we suppress love. If we suppress faith, we are also suppressing the joy of the Lord. We've got to get past some of our traditions, such as church is supposed to be very pious and quiet. A Spirit-led church is a place of healing, of deliverance, and like a hospital for the sick. It is also a place where we celebrate the victory of the Lord, and rejoice in the goodness of God. But if we suppress the joy of the Lord which springs up inside, it also suppresses love.

It is hard to love God when we are angry. It's even harder to love our spouse or our kids when we are angry. Come on, I'm talking to someone besides myself here! It's hard to love our pastor when we're angry, but he's telling the truth. When the joy is released, it brings the characteristic of love with it.

-

"As the Father loved Me, I have also loved you. Abide in My love. If you keep My commandments you will abide in My love, just as I have kept My Father's commandments and abide in His love. These things have I spoken to you that My joy may remain in you and your joy may be full." (John 15:9-11)

Jesus is speaking some very important principles in these verses, so our joy will be full. One is this: if we will follow the commands of the Lord, we will abide in love. When we release the joy of the Lord from our heart, the love of God will increase and become stronger. He wants His joy to remain in us, so that our joy will be full.

"This is My commandment that you love one another as I have loved you." (Verse 12)

Here is the key. When we release joy from our life, love will be imparted. Happy people like people! Have we ever seen an angry person give another person a hug and tell them they sure do love us? I have never seen that happen. I've never seen anyone with an angry spirit show love to another, and mean it with all their heart. They just do not have it within them because anger crowds out love. But when joy is in us, we want to love everyone. We could just hug everyone, because God is doing such exciting things in our life. We just want to hug this person and that person, because it is contagious.

"You love righteousness and hate wickedness, therefore God, Your God has anointed you with the oil of gladness more than your companions." (Psalm 45:7)

"Anointed" used here means the oil of gladness. When Jesse Duplantis came to preach in our church the first time, two persons on our staff happened to be in the foyer in the early afternoon at the same time when an automobile drove up. A lady jumped out of the car, ran over to our sign out front, and hugged it! She jumped back in her car and took off. When we have the joy of the Lord we want to hug everything! The staff noticed she had a North Dakota license plate. Obviously, they were excited they found the place where Jesse was going to be that evening.

2. Trust.

Joy produces trust. The joy in our heart results in

trust. "Trust" is firm belief in the honesty and the reliability of another. We are able to trust God without reservation when the joy of the Lord is strong in our spirit. We can trust His honesty, His truth, and His reliability. God is not going to speak anything to us that is untrue, or out of order. God will always speak to us along the lines of His Word. When we listen to that Word and receive it into our heart, trusting in the honesty, integrity, and the reliability of God, it causes confidence to rise from our spirit toward the Lord and His Word. Joy produces that kind of trust. "God, I know You've done this for me before and I know You can do it again! I know You touched me 20 years ago, and Lord, I know You can touch me now! I know You did a miracle for me in the past, and God, I know You can do a miracle for me again! I am trusting in You!" Trust increases and grows out of a spirit of joy and gladness.

"But let all those rejoice who put their trust in You. Let them ever shout for joy because You defend them. Let them also who love Your Name be joyful in You." (Psalm 5:11)

Look at that verse again. When God speaks into our day, we can have joy, and it produces trust and confidence in the Lord. When we get up in the morning we can tell Him, "I'm trusting You today, Lord! Do You know why? Your Word, number one. Your character of joy in my life, number two. I'm trusting You, Lord!"

The more we release joy from our heart, the greater

trust and confidence we have in the Lord. It just works that way. We think it should be the opposite. There are many things in Scripture which are separated from, different, and opposite from the world system. The world thinks one way, God instructs us another way. It may look like it is twisted up and backwards, but when the joy of the Lord is in our life, there will be increased trust in God. The more joy there is in my home the greater love and trust we have for our family members.

We like to have fun at our house. We aren't deadheads at home. My family and I don't live a different life at our house than we do on the platform. I was going to say this ugly face is the same in church as it is at home. But I won't, because I really am a handsome dude! At least that's what my wife tells me! But let me get back to this message.

We are talking about trust. Did you know that trust in God produces trust in others? The more joy we express, the more trust in the Lord. We trust His supernatural power. Say this aloud even though most of us can quote this next Scripture from memory:

"Trust in the Lord and do good. Dwell in the land and you shall feed upon His faithfulness. Delight yourself in the Lord and He will give you the desires of your heart. Commit your way to the Lord, trust also in Him and He shall bring it to pass." (Psalm 37:3-5)

Joy helps us trust. Trust in God produces trust in others, trust in the supernatural power of God, and trust in the Word of God, all by-products of joy expressed.

3. Favor.

Look in the mirror, right into your own eyes and say, "God favors me!" God releases His favor. There is divine favor when we live in joy. It doesn't do us any good to pout about things, or whine, "Nothing good ever happens to me!" Come on, you know what I'm talking about! We pull that on the Lord at times, while thinking we are really pious and holy. But do you know what? It stinks in the nostrils of God.

"What are you pouting about when I've given you joy?"

"Oh, God, you know that person over there has their financial needs met and mine aren't met!" "You know, that girl got to sing in front of the whole congregation. I have a better voice and I've never gotten to do that." Pouting doesn't get us anywhere with others or with God.

"Favor" is defined in the Word as regard, approval, or partial toward. God is partial towards us, people. Speak that aloud like you mean it! Joy produces the favor of God. It also means divine blessing and bestowment.

How do we think we are going to get into the blessings of God if we are pouting? We're not! If we're going to pout, we won't see favor. But if we say, "Okay, God,

I'm going to live in the joy of the Lord," we will see the blessings of God.

The rain falls on the just and the unjust (Matthew 5:45b). It doesn't matter what happens in the natural, we are to rejoice in Him. When we do, we have God's favor. When I complain, I've robbed myself of God's favor. If I pout, I'm also robbing myself of favor. But when I rejoice in the Lord, I have favor with God. Jesus had favor with God and men. God will give us favor with man as well, if we'll get out of the pouting and complaining and stay within the Spirit of joy. "God, You are filling me with the joy of the Lord in my heart. I thank You for joy! I can love You, I can trust You, and I have Your favor!"

"For You, O Lord, will bless the righteous with favor. You surround him as with a shield." (Psalm 5:12)

This verse follows up the last verse about trust. The Lord will encompass us about like a shield. He will give us favor, and surround us with Himself. In Proverbs 12:2, we are told, ***"A good man obtains favor from the Lord."*** We are obtaining favor from the Lord.

4. A Sound Mind.

"Sound mind" here means to be free from defect, damage, or decay. Satan wants to cause defect to us spiritually. He wants to cause us to decay and damage us, so we will not want to serve God again. That is his ploy. But here is the power of God at work: He gives us a sound mind.

"As a man thinks in his heart, so is he." (Proverbs 23:7)

There are so many blessings and benefits from our Lord when our lives line up with God's expectations for each believer. These are not unreachable goals, because He sees to it that His Word and His promises will accomplish what He sends them to do.

IN CONCLUSION

In closing, let me make clear the answer to the question, WHAT DOES GOD EXPECT OF US?

What God expects of believers He also empowers with His Spirit, so that you may fulfill His desire for you! As you submit (rank under His authority), and yield to Him (give away, surrender), His ability to carry it out will infuse your life. You CAN live in what God expects and empowers! Simply trust Him to work His work through you!